Wrestle To Win!

Wrestle To Win!

Be Smart. Be Ready.

Suggestions for improving your wrestling

Beasey S. Hendrix, III
A USA Wrestling <u>Gold Level</u> Certified Coach

High Performance Athletics
P.O. Box 669364
Marietta, Georgia 30066

10 9 8 7 6 5 4 3 2 1

ISBN   1-888397-00-4
LCCN   95-095287

Wrestle To Win!
Be Smart. Be Ready.
Suggestions for improving your wrestling

High Performance Athletics
P.O.Box 669364
Marietta, Georgia 30066

Thanks and Acknowledgements

I want to thank many people. Coach Dave LeBrande was my first real inspiration. He had a beautiful duckunder and a tremendous kid-based attitude. Robert Humphries was my first mentor.

And there are others. Coach Dariel Daniel allowed me the freedom to organize, experiment, and refine several programs, both athletic and mental. Drs. Don Mederios and Jim Barrell, psychology professors at West Georgia College in Carrollton, Georgia, listened, encouraged my studies, and asked the right questions.

Special thanks to some others:

Coaches Ron Gray and Steve Day for listening and suggesting. Brett Penager, from *USA Wrestling*, for his confidence and support. Betty Black and Melissa Keyes for editing. Wrestlers James Johnson, and Bobby Demerrit for sharing information and trying my programs. Doc Anderson for inviting me to teach my program at Troy State. Willie Hill for trusting me with his Morehouse Tiger Team.

To the 1995 USA World Greco Coach Dan Chandler, World place winner Matt Ghaffari and World Champion Dennis Hall for trusting my ideas.

I also owe so much to my athletes who put up with my approach. They allowed me to try things that were new. We didn't always agree, and some of them did not prosper, but to the athletes that have won thousands of medals, over a hundred state placings, dozens of All-American honors, and two World Championships, I say, "thanks".

To: TCHS, Troup, Cartersville, TSU, WGC, Morehouse College, the Wrestling USA family, my athletes: Big T, Flipper, Harvey, Clark, Big June, Eddie, Terry, Josh, Sean, Travis, Matt, Mike, Andy, Todd, Mitch, Edith, Gregg, Marcus and thousands of others!

Thanks a million!

VI   Wrestle To Win!

Table of Contents

Section I: Mental Skills For Wrestling

Section II: The Match

Photo Credits

Photographs on pages XIII, XIV, 54, and 174 are courtesy of **USA Wrestling**, Colorado Springs, Co.

Photographs on pages 53, and 90 are courtesy of **Wrestling USA Magazine**, Bozeman, MT.

Photograph on page 36 is courtesy of **Cartersville (GA) Daily Tribune**.

Photographs on pages 106, 112, 117, 118, 139, 140, and 158 are efforts of the author.

Photograph on page 97 is the effort of my friend Doug Reese.

Cover photo--James Johnson wins his third USA Wrestling National Greco-Roman Crown (1995). Courtesy of **USA Wrestling**.

Special thanks to **Cartersville Daily Tribune** for allowing a reprint of the article: *Mind Over Matter* by reporter Stephanie Ramage.

Introduction

Ready? That's usually the first word you hear after you shake hands. The referee asks, then blows the whistle. In practice the coach goes through the same ritual. It seems that everyone is asking if you are ready before they allow you to wrestle. Unfortunately, many of us are not. We have not learned how to prepare for competition. Yes, Coach taught us some moves and we think we know what is going on. Yes, we will step on the mat and give it our best. But, are we really ready?

What do we do?

How would you prepare a wrestler for competition? What topics would you teach? Just how does a wrestler learn the sport, and what, exactly, does one need to know?

Most of us learn through experience. We practice with other people and we listen to our coaches. These people show us moves and teach us how to get strong, and in shape. But, there is much more to the sport than just physical practice. Time and time again experts tell us how important mental skills are. They say, "Sport is at least 60% mental." or "Most of athletics is mental." Yet, very little of our practice time is devoted to mental skills. You drill your moves and you run. You do your push-ups. But do you focus on mental skills? Probably not.

That's the reason for this book!

Mental skills are overlooked by coaches and athletes. Even though most people agree that they are important, we still fail to devote any measurable time to the concept! "There is just not enough information." or "It is too hard to find" or "it takes too much time."

That's why I wrote this book, to help coaches and athletes improve their wrestling by increasing their mental skills. I wanted to share my 25 years of wrestling experience and to make the information available, in an easy-to-read form.

For the last decade, I have focused on mental skills. I have been researching and applying mental skills theories for coaches, wrestling teams, and wrestlers. Most coaches and athletes already have a good grasp of mental skills. They can tell me what happens to them before, during, and after matches. They describe the feelings and many can explain "problems" they encounter. Unfortunately, they don't have labels or names for what is happening to them.

Wrestle To Win! can help solve this problem. It focuses on mental, physical, and technical matters. See how the ideas fit your approach to wrestling. Use the good ideas. Throw the others away.

I have organized the book into sections set around loose themes. Within the sections are chapters. Each chapter is an article from a magazine. It is short and simple, and usually covers one topic. The chapters can be read in any order, and they are for both coaches and athletes.

So, check through the table of contents, pick out an article that interests you, then take a moment to read it. You will start to see that you already know so much about the sport. You just needed a little help in organizing your information. You will soon be able to take control of yourself and become that wrestler who really knows how to **Wrestle To Win!**

Physical skills and mental skills flow together to form the complete athlete. Here multi-time national champion James (JJ) Johnson works to control and lift his opponent, Army Greco star, Jerry Jackson.

Photo courtesy of USA Wrestling

Bobby Demeritt explodes with excitement after his 1994 Winter Championship victory over Shawn Sheldon. Note the difference in attitudes between the victor and the defeated warrior. (Sheldon came back to win the 1995 National Championship in Los Vegas, Nevada. His 7th National title.)

Photo courtesy of Casey Gibson and USA Wrestling

Section I

Mental Skills For Wrestling

Articles
1 **Sport Psychology For Wrestling**
2 **Competition**
3 **Activation, Focus, and Self-talk**
4 **Stress Reduction**
5 **Identifying Stress**
6 **Using Visualization**
7 **Mind Over Matter**
8 **Using Relaxation**

There are many basic mental skills necessary for athletes to be successful. These skills are not magic; they are just tools to use. Unfortunately, if you don't have these skills, your performances may be hindered. These articles give suggestions on how you can develop a set of mental skills that will enhance your performances.

The ideas of stress, anxiety, and nervousness and how they affect performances are discussed in the first three articles. These articles also introduce a basic vocabulary that will assist you in following the ideas outlined in later articles. From there we move into the mental skills and techniques that are used by successful athletes. Techniques and concepts are explained and demonstrated for you to examine and try.

Chapter 1

Introduction to Sport Psychology for Wrestling

Focus: What is sport psychology? Is it needed? What are some of its major concepts? How does it apply to wrestling?

If you were building the perfect wrestler, what skills would you include? Solid fundamentals and great moves? Strength and conditioning? What about drive and a burning desire to win?

When coaches and athletes discuss what it takes to make a successful wrestler, they debate many ideas. But just how often are psychological skills mentioned? And just where do mental skills fit in the task of building champion wrestlers or championship teams?

Wrestling is a demanding sport. It has all the worries that are present in other sports, plus the added pressures of being a martial art that pits individuals against one another. Add the tensions of weight control, and one has a sport that offers great opportunities for stress.

Demands of wrestling

Anyone who has ever been on the mat understands that there is much more to wrestling than just shooting moves and being in shape. The daily banging of practices and competition causes soreness, aches, and pains. "Cutting weight" can shorten tempers, and the constant threat of personal failure or injury can cause negative thoughts to surface.

Successful wrestlers ignore or control these negative

thoughts. For some it appears almost natural, as if they don't notice the darker side of competition. Others learn through experience and develop appropriate coping skills. But many wrestlers allow the negative side to become dominant in their thinking. This attitude can cause a drop in performance, and also affect the enjoyment level for those participants. But there is good news; we have the information and skills that can be employed to help control negative pressures and improve performances.

Mental skills

Most coaches and athletes probably agree that mental skills are important. But the idea of using sport psychology concepts to organize mental skills practices may be a new or controversial idea for some. There is resistance to the idea of sport psychology. Thoughts of others "messing with their heads" often cause concern for athletes, while another problem for them is the lack of organized sport psychology programs. The basic information is available, but it is often presented in a complicated, fragmented, and non-sport-specific fashion, or it may stay hidden deep within the computer data bases. If we can reach past these problems, we will see that there are several important concepts that wrestlers can use to develop better mental skills. Probably the most important idea is that there are two major application methods for sport psychology.

The first application method can be labeled an "educational" or "developmental" method. Mental skills are learned as part of the total wrestling skills package. Like stand-ups, double legs, and bridges, these skills are included as fundamentals.

We can identify two groups of educational topics. One is strategies; in which the wrestler learns the basic rules of playing. (No upper body with a big lead. Keep your head up on bottom. Take hand control on bottom. Work for set-ups when on your feet.) The other educational application is performance enhancement; in which the athlete is taught how to handle psychological concerns that may arise during the course of the season. In this process, wrestlers are taught how to concentrate, how to control doubt, and how to avoid common mental errors that might cause problems in practice or a match. Both strategy and performance enhancement techniques are easily applied to group situations, and can be used with individuals, small groups, or the whole team.

The second application method is called "intervention", or "corrective" psychology. Unfortunately, this is the style most often connected with performance psychology; an athlete is diagnosed with a performance related problem and is "corrected by therapy". This method tends to be individual-based, and is the least time and cost effective.

No matter which method you feel is best, there are some basic mental skills that should be included in any wrestler's training. Motivation and goal setting are good introductory skills. Learning theory and visualization can be used to improve practice time, while focus and self-talk can be worked on daily to assist with stress control. The amount of work, and the topics you want emphasized can be tailored to meet any team's or individual's needs.

Practicing mental skills

Mental skills can be learned, but they must be practiced to improve. They appear to follow the same learning curve as physical skills and can be practiced using the same techniques. To successfully use a mental skill, you must: A) introduce the skill, B) practice it, C) become so efficient that it is ingrained into memory, becomes automatic, and is forgotten.

With practice schedules already filled, when do wrestlers have time to practice these additional tasks? There are ways to incorporate these skills without demanding additional time from the athletes, as much of the work can be performed during practice. Warm-ups, cool-downs, skull sessions, or conditioning periods offer excellent times to practice mental skills. The topics may be covered as athletes perform other tasks.

So, whether you are a coach or an athlete, there are skills that you can use to enhance performances and improve the enjoyment of your sport. By understanding, then utilizing the concepts and ideas behind sport psychology, you can learn the mental skills before you actually need them. (Just like learning to counter the half nelson before you need it in a match!? Practice the skills until they become so ingrained that you don't think about them. Then if problems arise, redirect or correct them.

Remember--**Matches are won by hard work and solid preparation, but they are often lost because of poor psychological skills, or mental errors.**

Key thoughts:

1. Mental skills are useful to every athlete.

2. Mental skills should be learned as part of your training.

3. There are methods to correct mental errors or problems.

4. You can use mental skills to improve your performances.

5. Sport psychology is just the idea that we think during athletic performances.

Chapter 2

Competition: Enjoying A Stressful Situation

Focus: Why do kids have a good time playing in backyard sports, yet often become stressed out when they enter organized games? What is flow? How does competition affect an athlete?

Organized competition is stressful for many athletes, and that is normal. Competition can produce stress. The uncertainty of outcome, fear of failure, and numerous other concerns can cause athletes to experience nervousness and anxiety. Yet, when we think about our earliest sports experiences, we can recall little or no stress. Why is this so?

Most of us enter athletics by participating in neighborhood games. We learn to compete in a situation that is usually organized and supervised by children.

Take a moment and think about these games. The teams were selected by the players. Care was taken to keep competition fair. The games were officiated and even scored by the participants. Were these games stressful? Did you get nervous or uptight thinking about your performances or the outcome? Probably not.

Now, think about competition in an organized sports program. Do you become nervous? Do you worry about your performances and the results? Many people do, and that is something that sport psychologists, coaches, and athletes are trying to understand. What are the differences between play and organized sport activities in regard to mental stress?

Kid's games versus organized sports

One of the most popular theories is based around the concept of time. We find that children tend to stay in the now or in the present when they play. They concentrate on having fun and enjoying the process, the actual playing of the game. Very little thought is given to the questions that ask: What will happen if? What will so and so think? How will I do? No, kids just play and enjoy the moment.

This changes when we enter organized athletics. Results become very important and the actual competition becomes of secondary importance. Athletes begin to change their focus from the process of playing, to anxiously awaiting the results. In other words, the final score becomes more important than how we play the game. Some athletes begin to live in the future, focusing on and worrying about how they will do.

Preparing for competition

That brings us to an interesting problem. We organize our practice and training programs based upon our past performances. We look at the skill level of the athlete and use recent performances as feedback for developing a work-out program. Then we direct the athletes towards improving future performances. Almost all of our work is centered around the two periods in time that we can't control--the past and the future. Yet, when we compete, we are placed into a situation that is 'now', in the present, not the past or future. But athletes have very little training in handling the pressures of now, so they often feel nervous or uneasy when it's time to compete.

State anxiety

Some stress is normal. Competition is a judgement situation and it tends to cause anxiety. As a matter of physiology, a little nervousness helps prepare us for competition by activating our natural defense system. We become more aware, and our body readies itself for fight or flight. So, nervousness in itself is not a bad thing.

We call this nervousness caused by the setting or situation--state anxiety.

Let's look at some examples. Each of the following situations could cause a case of state anxiety, and there are several concerns that might add to the stress production. Just what could be causing this anxiety? By looking at each situation we might be able to pinpoint some of these stress producing thoughts.

1. You are a heavyweight. You wrestle last. Your team is ahead by 2 points, and has a 25 match winning streak. It is time for you to take the mat.

This heavyweight is in a pressure situation. He may feel that the team and even the whole community is counting on his performance. How will he feel if he lets them down? What will the team and community think of him? How will his girlfriend and parents react? This may be what he is actually thinking about before his match. We often find athletes focusing on a fear of failure, and the opinions of significant others when thrown into this type of situation.

2. You are wrestling a two-time state champ who has pinned 15 in a row. He also has a 30 match winning streak.

Wrestling a state champion is always tough, but a two-timer. Wow? It would be hard not to focus on our opponent's ability when he has such an impressive set of credentials. It is in this type of situation that we often see wrestlers shift their focus to what their foe has done. These wrestlers become so involved with their opponent's reputation that they forget to develop a plan of their own. They enter a match with no idea of direction. This uncertainty handicaps their performances, and the athletes often appear sluggish or lost until they have some success and get a series going.

3. Your team wrestles a tough team this week. The number one man turns his ankle? You are asked to make weight and wrestle tomorrow.

As we know, injuries could suddenly change a season. Unexpected, they can place an athlete or a team into an immediate pressure situation. Our substitute will probably be faced with some uncertainty and fear. Will he be able to make weight? Who will he be wrestling? When are we leaving? What do I need? His day will become filled with questions that need answers.

Trait anxiety

Most athletes in these situations would probably have negative thoughts and ideas pop into their minds. That would be normal. It is a defense mechanism that allows humans to make decisions and redirections. If we didn't notice the problems that were arising, we would not be able to survive in a constantly changing environment. The key to any pressure situation is to note the negative thought; evaluate it, quickly find a solution; then move on. If the negative thought is irrational or unimportant, refocus and get back to a more productive line of thought and action.

Unfortunately, there are athletes who produce a large amount of pressure because of their particular personality. These persons are labeled as having trait anxiety. State anxiety causes enough stress in athletes, but when the wrestler is also trait anxious, the problems multiply. Why is this so? Because we have pressure-producing people placed in pressure-producing situations. Boom! It is too much. They feel a double whammy.

How do we wrestle these anxieties?

There is no easy fix, but there are some things you can do to attempt to help control your emotion. First, find the <u>now</u> in your performance. You have prepared and now it is time to do. Learn to narrow your focus to the present. Think: *What do I need to be doing right now?* Form a plan of action, then say to yourself, "This is what I need to be doing, right now." Make your self-talk statements positive, active, and goal directed. Some of your self-talk statements will center around the near future (Post his arms, drop my level, then shoot a double.), but this is okay since it has to do with your plans for the match.

Control your focus. Constantly scan for new information. Know the score and plan your strategy. Check the competition and be aware of his position. Where are you on the mat? How is your position? What should you be doing now? There is so much to think about. It will take all of your training and competitive experience to be able to perform successfully. If you are properly focused on your performance, you won't have time to worry about the outcome.

Coaches can help their athletes through these anxious moments by offering positive statements. Focus on your athlete's needs. Help him make a plan of action that is built around his abilities and training? Avoid telling him what not to do. "Watch our for his double leg", only focuses him on a problem. Try to help him work his series. "Remember, Jimmy. Good stance, nice motion, drop your level. Your duck has been working well. Inside control, window, penetrate. Work your stuff. You be the man." This helps Jimmy get started. After the match begins, he will probably open up and get into a good series.

Understanding flow

This brings us to a concept called *flow*. *Flow* is the state or condition that one enters when challenges, skill, and enjoyment all blend together. A person in flow often loses the sense of time and is not really aware of himself as a person. He or she becomes part of the experience. It may sound strange, but let us look at what we are trying to understand.

Have you ever become so involved in doing something that you became unaware of anything else. You become so involved that it feels like a dream. Maybe you were driving and became hypnotized by the road. Maybe you were watching a movie, or were at a party. What about your best match? You probably remember the feeling. (Professor Mahayli Csikszentmihali calls it an *optimal experience*.)

This is the type of feeling or situation that we are

trying to achieve when we compete. Focus our attention, use our skills, and reach that level where everything begins to flow. We do not worry about the future or past, we just get into the match and let our training take over. If we do things right and have a little luck, we will enter flow.

As an athlete, there are some things you can do to encourage the flow state. You can work to reach flow by concentrating on what you are trying to accomplish. In practice, attack and shoot your moves. Try your series and force you partner to react. Get after them and have fun. Learn to enjoy the wrestling. After all, we practice much more than we compete.

Coaches can help get athletes into flow by allowing flurries to continue without over-coaching. (How many flurries have been broken to point out someone's foot was misplaced? It is a sin that we all do.) Allow the wrestlers to keep wrestling. Obviously they are having fun, wrestling hard, and getting into shape. What more do we want? If they all would practice like that, they would be almost unbeatable!

Performance jitters

There are times when things go badly. We run into a problem then get stuck somewhere between concern and panic. What should we do when we encounter a sudden problem? When unexpected or bad events occur, we immediately shift our focus to that concern. It is part of the defense system we mentioned earlier.

Wrestling offers many situations that can result in these problems. What are some of the most common? They are not secrets; you have seen them all. 1) The referee makes a ridiculously bad call. 2) You slip as you lower your level to shoot. 3) You blow a move. 4) You get tossed to your back late in the match.

Successful athletes and teams understand that these things do happen. They talk about these situations and develop plans to lessen or overcome their impact. These successful people learn to shift gears back to the present.

They think, "What should I be doing right now to recover from this and get back into the match?"

Hints

If you encounter stress that causes you to lose focus or start having negative talk, understand that it is normal and sometimes even helpful. It makes you work to focus on problems that might go unnoticed. If this causes you to find solutions, then it is okay. It is actually beneficial for you.

But, just thinking about your nervousness will not help; so, note the anxieties; then, direct your attention to goals and solutions. Think about what you need to be doing to be successful; then, do it. Like the little boy playing in the backyard game, play your best and enjoy the game. Narrow your concentration to the present and become so involved with the positive side of your performance that you enter a *flow state*. Afterwards, evaluate your performance, set adjusted goals, make desired corrections, then savior your performance.

There is much so of the positive that we can savor. Make sure you take the time to enjoy your successes. Often we get lost with the idea that we did not place highly enough, or that so and so had a better day. That attitude is one that is living in the past, and we can not afford to spend much time dwelling on negative memories. Try to remember the positive and look forward to your upcoming match. It is the next time you will be able to use the wrestling skills that you have worked so hard to develop.

Chapter 3

Activation, Focus, and Self-talk

Focus: Nervous, you talk to yourself, thinking about the match. You feel your excitement build. You often use focus, self-talk, and activation, you just don't know it.

Many things can affect a wrestler's performance. Physical concerns such as conditioning, health, weight control, technical skill level, and even the amount of practice time contribute to a performance. Mental aspects such as levels of excitement, topics of focus, and types of self-talk can also have tremendous impact upon how a wrestler performs in any given match. Wrestlers and coaches want to be ready to perform well. But, knowing how to mentally prepare for a match can be a tricky process. It involves several concepts that are easy to understand, but are rarely formally taught by coaches.

Goldilocks and the three bears

The first major concept that we need to understand is *activation*, sometimes called *arousal*. Many sport psychologists and coaches use the terms "activated" and "aroused" when discussing how excited a wrestler is before a match, but what do these terms actually mean? Performance theory proposes that an athlete has an optimum or "best" level of nervousness or excitement. If he is too relaxed (mentally too cold), he responds slowly and his performance levels dip. If he is too nervous (mentally too hot), he becomes jittery and overloaded with worries. He can lose focus, and his performance may suffer.

We have all heard of the athlete who was "dead" before a match, or of one who "choked", but what do these terms mean, and what do wrestlers need to know to understand the process of preparing for competition? The easiest way is to explain this concept is to recall the story of Goldilocks and the Three Bears. Just like Goldie and her porridge, wrestlers must find that point where their arousal is "just right".

Too hot, or too cold

Picture yourself in a deep sleep. Would you be able to wrestle well? Heck no! You wouldn't be able to react. What if you were sleepy? You would be slow to react, and your decision-making system would not be in full force. It would be like you were too cold, or not ready.

This has happened to many wrestlers. They enter the match too relaxed. Some are overconfident, and not really thinking about what they need to do to wrestle well. Others might have been casually focusing on another topic, and not been warmed-up when their turn to compete arrived. Sometimes the structure of a tournament or meet catches athletes in this predicament, as when a mat assignment is changed, or a schedule is altered to speed up the competition.

But what about being "too hot"? Picture yourself getting so excited that you start to breathe hard, your heart beat accelerates, and you feel like you are going to have a heart attack or stroke. Could you perform? Again, the answer is no! Yet, many wrestlers put themselves into this position by focusing on topics that they can't control, or by worrying about subjects that are inappropriate. This over-activation is common in wrestling. Athletes often talk themselves into anxieties by looking at their opponents' big arms, comparing won-loss records, or even judging a foe's ability by the tradition of his school.

So being too nervous, or too calm can actually cause performances to suffer. To be at their best, wrestlers must learn to control arousal, and keep the excitement at a level that is "just right" for optimal performance.

But how can we do this? There are two psychological skills that athletes can employ to help control anxieties. These skills are already used by every wrestler. With a little practice, they can be improved to allow the athletes to gain better control of their activation.

Two mental skills

The first skill is called *focus. Focus* is the ability to concentrate or think about the important topics, while blocking out or ignoring unneeded thoughts. We use this skill daily, and it allows us to compete in a complicated environment. At a match, good focus allows a wrestler to shift attention from the crowd, to an opponent. It also helps the athlete to ignore a battle that is taking place on a nearby mat, or a public address announcement that occurs during his match. Without focus, the world would offer too much stimulation; we could never stay on task.

Unfortunately, some individuals suffer from poor, or inappropriate focus, and this can cause added anxiety and a resulting over-arousal. They tend to focus on the negative aspects of the competition and look at the problems they perceive.

But there are some ways to improve focus. First, realize what you are thinking about. Will it help prepare you for your match? Does it center around something you can change or control? You should try to focus on topics that will aid you in planning or performing. Then relax and wait, or plan your strategies, focusing on whatever you feel will enhance your mental state.

The second skill is called *self-talk*. Self-talk is the discussion that athletes have with themselves. It can affect how you feel, and how you wrestle. Self-talk can be positive (I'm going to kill him.), negative (Man, is he huge.) or neutral (I need this takedown to win.). Negative thinking lowers your expectations and can actually help your foe. (I'll never take him down.? So, work towards positive comments that you believe (My lateral drop has been awesome!), or neutral statements that focus on a specific task (He's open for a double.)

Using all 3 skills

These are mental skills, so to improve them we must think about what we are thinking about? First, recognize your focus. Is it appropriate? Concentrate on topics that will enable you to improve. Planning is better than worry. If your focus strays, redirect it and get back on track. Next, evaluate your self-talk. Is it positive or neutral? It should be. If it is negative, then stop it and try to start some new, task-oriented thinking. Check your arousal state. Are you ready to perform? If you are properly focused and your self-talk is right, your arousal level will probably be okay.

Practice these skills. Like physical skills, they improve with training. Decide what you need to think about, and how you need to phrase the thoughts. By controlling these two processes, you are gaining control of your emotions, and enhancing your athletic ability.

Conclusions

Wrestlers can be too relaxed or too nervous. They must work to find the proper middle ground. They can learn to control emotional energy by understanding the concept of focus, and by directing their attention to appropriate topics. An effort should also be made to control self-talk, keeping it positive or neutral.

These mental skills are easy to use, but athletes must make a conscious effort to identify, then change any inappropriate thinking. By controlling their arousal levels, athletes can enter a match ready to compete, and be better able to perform at their optimum level. If you notice arousal problems, if you are too activated, or if you are not ready to perform, check your focus. What are you thinking about? What is your self-talk centering on? If it is something that will help you, then you are okay. If your thoughts are interfering with your preparation, then redirect them and move toward a solution.

Chapter 4

Stress Reduction and Anxiety Control

⸻

Focus: What is stress? How does it affect us? What happens when we are stressed? Can we gain control of anxiety and stress?

⸻

"What will he try? Sometimes he shoots doubles; other times he goes upper body. What if he throws in a leg ride? Last time I couldn't get up for the whole period. Dad said I looked paralyzed. I can't let that happen again."

There it is again, that feeling of doubt and worry. Stress, anxiety, nerves, fear; it wears many names and has many causes. One thing is for certain, it affects many wrestlers.

Friend and enemy

Some anxiety is good for competition. It makes a wrestler alert, and helps activate the body. But an athlete can become too anxious, or too nervous, and his ability to wrestle can suffer.

There are many things that can cause an athlete to become over-stressed, but most problems are caused by inappropriate focus and negative self-talk. Often an athlete will begin to focus on problems or concerns. This results in self-talk that is based on uncertainty or failure. Plans are soon forgotten or are consumed by this anxiety. This negative focus can become an obsession that controls the wrestler's thinking, leaving him overloaded with questions and unsure of his next step.

Topics of concern

Doctor Jim Barrell, West Georgia College professor and sport psychologist for several professional teams, says, "Athletes often suffer from uncertainty of outcome, and the fear of failure. They can also begin to worry about the opinions of others. These thoughts cause the athletes to focus on outside concerns, taking them away from objectives that will help their performances. It makes them waste time and energy on worry, and often produces unneeded pressure. The athlete's thinking shifts from the task that he wants to accomplish, to actually doubting it can be done."

"This uncertainty of outcome, fear of failure, and concern for the opinions of other people actually encourages the wrestlers to have self-doubt. It attacks their self confidence and causes frequent restructuring of plans and goals," adds Barrell.

Shifts in thinking

When wrestlers focus on these anxiety-producing topics, they tend to focus on the future. Unfortunately, no one can control the future, so it is filled with unknowns. These unknowns help produce more questions, which in turn produce more stress. A circle of anxiety develops.

In trying to deal with these unknowns, some athletes become overly cautious. Instead of making self-referenced, task-related goals, they become reactionary, waiting on others to move. But by waiting for others to act, the wrestlers put themselves into another stressful situation and encourage even more uncertainty. With some individuals, this stress becomes so great that it actually interferes with the physical performance. The wrestlers appear to "freeze up" and are often labeled as "chokers", "front runners" or "losers".

How to control the stress

Sport psychology offers several methods that can help control performance-based stress. Relaxation and visualization are two of the most common, and they are often first used as intervention strategies. In relaxation, an athlete learns to control stress by following a system of muscle drills, teamed with calming thoughts. In visualization the athlete reduces anxiety by mentally picturing himself being successful in different situations.

These two methods are coping skills that can help reduce any stress that is produced by performance anxiety. They are easy to learn and use. If these skills are practiced regularly as part of a mental skills program, they can become performance enhancers that really work.

A quick relaxation session might include:
A) learning to control your breathing, B) focusing on positive ideas, or C) focusing on successfully completing tasks. It may even include a version of progressive relaxation where you flex and relax your major muscle groups. By overloading your muscles with a tight flex, then relaxing, you reframe the way your mind is perceiving its tension. You can then focus on calm and relaxing thoughts.

Learning visualization is easy. You really just have to learn to control your daydreams since that is what visualization resembles. Work to get control of vividness, size, and pace of action. The major difference between visualization and day-dreaming is that when you visualize, you are consciously trying to control your visualization.

The use of a band aid approach is appropriate when time is short, such as at a game, or in mid-season. In these situations, there is just not enough time to work through any problems. You must do the best you can in a short period of time.

But if time is not a problem or constraint, psychologists encourage a more permanent solution, suggesting that athletes change their thinking patterns that cause these anxieties. This change can occur if the athlete works on specific tasks. They recommend:

1)   Become task-oriented and self-referenced. Learn to plan matches around your abilities and your goals. Decide what you do well, and focus on your strengths.

2) Shift your plan of action to the present. Decide what you need to do to improve your performance and then begin. "I will" becomes "I am".

3) Do it. Take charge of the situation ad attempt to complete your plans.

4) If problems arise, find the solutions, adjust, then get right back on your new goals.

Another popular technique that is much like relaxation is called centering. It consists of focusing your attention on a spot that is inside your body. The athlete uses this centered spot to as a focal point of awareness. *Centering* uses breath control as a key or trigger. Anytime a wrestler has a moment's break, he should draw in a deep breath and refocus.

Some experts suggest that the wrestler engage in a self-talk dialog that helps him to refocus. Words such as *relax, recover, let's do it,* can assist the athlete in returning to the present.

Positive and task oriented

Coaches can help discourage stress by employing positive teaching styles. They can remove the concept of "countering" and encourage the completion of moves. An anxiety-based coach might teach, "When a man shoots a double leg, sprawl back quickly to counter his penetration. Don't let him get in deep, or you're in trouble". A positive, task-based coach might say, "When a man shoots in on a double, he has left his good stance. We can take advantage of his motion by redirecting his attack, making an angle, then turning the corner. Punish him for leaving his stance. Get that takedown!"

The positive coach focuses his athletes' attention on scoring and being successful instead of worrying about the opponent's success. Good coaches make their athletes see the best opportunities for success, and then encourage the athletes to complete the task. These coaches avoid negative instructions. They stay away from "don'ts", and teach the wrestlers what to do.

Don't worry if you are using don't! Everyone uses the

word when teaching or thinking about what to do. Just make sure you follow any "don'ts" with an instruction that tells the athlete what to do. Give a positive and clear instruction. This positive direction helps remove fear and allows the athlete to stay goal directed.

An example of this would be: When I work with teams, I often see young coaches teaching a drop step or some type of leg attack. They will instruct the youngster in the proper technique, then allow the athlete to practice the skill. If the athlete does something wrong, the coach may say, "Don't step like this." They show the athlete what not to do. The "don't" statement needs to be followed with a correct example, an example of what the coach wants accomplished. "Don't step outside, that takes you away from the opponent. Turn your foot around and behind like this.", is a better way to teach. The coach used the "don't" approach but finished it with a good direction.

It is the same for the athletes. A stressful prematch focus and self-talk might be: "My single hasn't been working. What will I do now? If I shoot and don't get in, he may cross face me and spin behind. Then what will everyone think? I hardly ever give up a takedown."

Instead of focusing on what you can't do, focus on what you need to do. Stop worrying about things you can't control. Concentrate and stay on task. A positive thinking, task-oriented wrestler might say, "I'm going with my single leg. I've had a little trouble lately, but I can correct that. Good stance, movement, drop my level, then explode. Shoot through him. Good penetration. Yes, that will get it."

Move away from uncertainty and that fear of failure. Shift your attention away from what might happen and what others might think. Take control and remind yourself of performance cues. Keep thinking in the present, ready to act. By focusing on your plans and techniques, you keep your thoughts on the topics you control. You use your mental energies on things that will help the performance.

Conclusion

Stress is a complicated and involved state of mind. It has many causes and can affect performances in many ways.

There are methods for controlling excessive stress that can be learned and used by wrestlers. Relaxation and visualization are common techniques that are employed to battle stress.

The best method for controlling anxiety is to control focus and self-talk. In using this method, wrestlers learn to focus on positive, self-referenced goals and to work in the present to accomplish their objectives. Thoughts of failure, uncertainty, and significant others are replaced with plans for success. The athletes then follow these plans to reach their goals. If questions or problems arise, the athlete focuses on finding solutions.

Coaching styles can affect anxiety levels, and coaches and athletes must learn to identify and use the mental skills that will enhance their ability to perform.

After the initial contact, most wrestlers settle into their match. By practicing positive self-talk, athletes can learn to control much of their match anxiety.

Chapter 5

Identifying
and
Controlling Stress

Focus: What are the different types of stress? Are there different ways of controlling them? Is all stress bad? How does stress affect our thinking?

You are standing behind the team bench, awaiting your match. Your body is tense. You notice that thoughts of doom are beginning to run through your mind, so you start to get a little nervous. You don't like the feeling. It causes you to have some uneasiness. What can you do?

There are several things that sport psychologists recommend for controlling stress and anxiety. Some methods are long range attempts at restructuring thinking patterns. These take organized practice and a large investment of time. Other methods focus on quick relief that enables an athlete to just get through the competition. These methods are often referred to as "band-aid" approaches because they only mask or cover the real problem.

Unfortunately, the time restraints of a season can put restrictions on the amount of time that an athlete can devote to learning a mental skill. Most athletes want to know the quickest and best ways to handle any anxieties that might pop into a dual match or tournament setting. They really don't have the time to worry about the underlying cause of their stress; they need help and they need it at that moment. With respect to that thought, let's look into some quick and effective methods for putting a band-aid on that mental sore!

Effects of stress

Stress affects wrestlers in different ways. Some sense a nervous feeling in their body. They begin to feel "uptight", "tense", or "frozen". Others begin to notice negative talk floating into their thinking. They can't seem to shake those ideas of worry or dread.

The bad news is that both of these types of stress can affect your performances. Each type can eat at you and cause a shift in focus, from completing the task to focusing on the obstacle or problem. But there is some good news. There are methods we can employ that will help to calm or control both types.

1. *Somatic* (body) stress is when you react physically to a situation. The body becomes tense in reaction to a perceived danger. A diagram of this type of stress would show the body reacting first, then triggering anxiety and poor performances.

Bodily Stress--> Anxiety--> Performance Problems

The most common and easiest method of stopping this physical tension is the use of deep breathing exercises, centering, or relaxation methods. (An example of a relaxation script is included later in this chapter.)

2. With *cognitive stress* (negative thinking) the wrestler builds anxiety by thinking negatively about an event or task. These thoughts cause physical symptoms that may interfere with an athlete's performance. The key to stopping this type of nervousness is to stop the negative thoughts, then move on to positive or neutral thinking. It sounds easy, but it can be hard to train yourself to stop, then refocus. A diagram of this type of stress would show negative thoughts occurring first, then bodily stress forming that could interfere with performance.

**Negative thoughts->Bodily Stress->
Performance Problems**

Somatic stress

If your body shows signs of somatic stress first, try to control your physical symptoms by relaxing. The easiest method is to take control of your breathing. Take a deep breath and slow down. If that doesn't work, a short version of a relaxation script may be all you need.

Some programs suggest that you use this relaxation system before you enter any type of situation that you feel will be stressful. They suggest that you calm yourself down before you begin to feel tense. Train yourself to go through a quick edition of your favorite relaxation script anytime you foresee an upcoming, tense situation. Use the relaxation to prepare yourself to enter the setting. This will stop the tension from beginning.

This sounds good. If you have the awareness or discipline to incorporate this approach into your system, it is a good strategy. Just beware the habit of becoming too calm. Make sure you can control your activation.

How would you use these techniques?

It is easy. When you think or feel that you are entering a stressful situation, recognize the fact, then take a moment to gain control by starting your stress reduction techniques. Stress comes from within, so you are the one who is in control. Just learn to assert yourself and take control of your body's reactions. If you can develop a short personal script that you can use, it will probably be best. You might want to say something like: "Okay, I'm starting to feel a little tense. I need to get control. Slow down. Take a breath. Relax. Think about (something you think is relaxing). That's better"

The key is for you to understand that <u>you can control your stress</u>. By employing a stress-reduction technique before the anxiety takes control, you win the battle without having to fight. (If you can't design your own set of thoughts, then use the relaxation script found at the end of this chapter.)

You may also want to use your stress control as you leave a stressful situation. This will help you relax and be able to transfer into your next activity without suffering from any lingering anxiety. By calming down and relaxing afterward, you improve your focus and will help yourself recover from the physical stresses of practice or competition.

Negative thoughts

Negative thinkers--wrestlers whose thoughts tend to wander towards negative ideas or concerns, can apply a negative thought-stopping strategy to help control the problem. This will help stop the stress from taking the next step and affecting your body. You do this by first identifying the negative thoughts, then redirecting your thinking to what you want to be doing now. Learn to get into the present and do what you need to do, instead of focusing on worries or negative concerns.

Most athletes tell me that they feel stressed-out when their minds begin to focus on negative thoughts or ideas. "I can't." "I'll never." "I don't think..." "But what if...?" These are NEGATIVE SELF-TALK STATEMENTS, and they will work against you in your pursuit of good performances and fun. Basically, any thinking or talking that causes you to move away from your goal is "bad", and you must correct or redirect this thinking by following three steps.

1) Realize. We must identify negative self-talk. Remember, it is any thinking that focuses on worry, doubt, or failure. Recognize any negative thoughts that enter your thinking. Then, admit that you are negative talking--that you are negging out, and starting to defeat yourself. Once you identify the negative thoughts, you can start to take corrective measure.

2) *Stop it! Stop the negative.* Make yourself stop. Say, "I am being negative--I've got to stop. It will not help. It will only hurt if I keep thinking this way." It sounds easy, but it takes an effort to stop this process. Some folks suggest that you say "STOP!" aloud to trigger or cue yourself to change the behavior. This action or word will give you a moment to collect yourself.

3) *Redirect your thoughts.* This is a skill that you must work on to become effective. If you just say "stop!",

chances are that you will return right back to your previous line of thinking, and your tension will continue to build. You must learn to self-talk yourself into positive or neutral thinking. Think, "What should I be focusing on right now?" "What can I be doing that will help me?" "What should I be doing right now?" If you are able to come up with an answer, then shift to that task and get back into the groove. If you can't think of anything, then just shift your thoughts to your task and get going.

Closing

So, decide which type of stress affects you the most, then begin to practice one of the controlling methods. It won't be hard; it will just take a little time and patience.

After you begin to feel confident in your knowledge and skill with the methods, you will be able to apply them in real life situations. The key is to recognize the stress before it builds, decide what type of stress it is, then shift into your control strategy. That sounds pretty easy, and it actually is.

Short Relaxation Script

This script simply shows you how to use a physical relaxation method. The major ideas are to relax your body, clear your mind, then focus on the physical sensations. It is not magic, so don't expect any miracles. It is a method that many people find will help, but it takes concentration and a little work. If you take the time to practice and master this method of relaxing, you can develop your own system that will be even more effective. Remember: *practice makes perfect*! That goes for mental skills as well as physical ones.

So--

Find a comfortable place to sit or lie down. Make sure it is a safe area and that you are not driving or doing anything that needs total focus.

Shut your eyes. Let your shoulders relax and drop down. Allow your head to fall forward. Take a deep breath, then blow it out, slowly. Take another and blow it out. Imagine all of your stress and worries leaving your body with that long breath. Blow it out as far as possible.

Clear your mind of any worries or thoughts. Concentrate on the feeling of heaviness that you now have in your hands and feet. Begin to notice the pressure points where your body is touching the floor or chair. Your head touches. Your back touches. Your hips touch. Your calves. Your heels. You begin to feel as if the floor or couch is lifting you up. So heavy that you are sinking into the floor.

Take another deep breath. Think of something that you enjoy or that makes you feel good. Now, see yourself doing that activity. You feel very relaxed and calm. You watch yourself doing the activity as you get even heavier. Hear the sounds. Smell the odors. Feel the sensations.

Enjoy this calm feeling. If you want to drift away, then allow yourself the enjoyment. Let your thoughts drift. You can stay awake as you move through a series of pleasant thoughts, feelings, and scenes.

You now feel very relaxed and calm--more relaxed than ever before. Focus on the task you want to accomplish and keep your self-talk positive or task-based. Enjoy this calm feeling. Let this feeling spread across your body. Let it control your thoughts and continue until you have completed your image.

You are now ready. Open your eyes, stretch and go on to your next activity.

If you notice any more bodily tension, take a moment to run through the relaxation break. It won't take long, and you will soon be controlling that uneasy feeling that you once experienced.

Chapter 6

Visualization:
For Stress Control
And Performance Enhancement

Focus: What is visualization? How do we use it? Is there more than one method? What is imagery? Simulation?

Picture this

I looked across the mat toward my opponent. A collegiate national champion, he was favored to win this tournament. I had never really seen him before, but I had heard stories about his size. At 6' 6" and over 440 pounds, he was a real monster, and now I had to wrestle him. He walked up to the mat, his red singlet shining in the light. Red? For some reason I thought about a bull! A sense panic shot through my mind. What could I do? He was so dead gum big!

I remember saying to myself, "Wait a minute. You better get a plan. Take a second and think about what we need to do." I don't know why I was using the word 'we'. I guess my mind was talking to my body, but it didn't really matter. I knew what the voice meant, so I began to form a plan.

I thought for a minute. "I need to turn the corners. I'll post his shoulders, shuck an arm, then beat him on the outside." I shut my eyes and formed a picture in my mind. *Stance, contact, arm shuck, penetrate, turn that corner, get control.* I saw myself being successful and the panic loosened its grip. I had a plan. Now I could focus on my series and stop worrying about his. I had visualized my success and had refocused my attention on what I needed to do.

Hot topic

Visualization is a hot topic in sport psychology. It is promoted as a method that can be used to improve performances. Athletes are being encouraged to imagine, envision, or even 'just think about' performances as an aid in preparing for their competitions. But what is visualization? What does it do? How is it done?

In the simplest of definitions, *visualization* is daydreaming, or imagining oneself in a performance. It is a simple process, and most people visualize things throughout their life. Some of you may remember thinking about what you were going to say to that girl you wanted to call. You "sorta practiced" what you were going to say. Others may remember a time when you had to make up a story to tell to your parents. You wanted to stay out of trouble so you "figured out" a story to tell them. If you have done either of these tasks, you probably visualized the scene while making your plans.

People visualize in different ways. Some claim to "see", others use all of their senses, while a few claim to "hear" or "just know". Even if they don't know that it is called "visualization", most athletes already understand and accept the idea. That makes it easy to implement the skill within a program. (I often joke my teacher friends by telling them that teachers are the best instructors of visualization. I point out that most of us have tuned out a teacher and engaged in some sort of visualization or daydream.)

Introducing visualization

To encourage my athletes to use the skill, I begin by having them close their eyes and think about their home. They then open their eyes and draw a sketch of the house. Most have no problem, although some claim they never imagined the building, they just "remembered it".

There are athletes who have trouble with the concept of visualization and are not responsive. They usually can visualize a scene, but they resist admitting it. As a convincer, I have them describe their favorite car or the perfect girl. Many of the doubters smile when they realize that they are describing something that is not there. After a while, they usually admit they can do it, but some say they don't see how it will help them prepare for matches.

The key to using in visualization is to remember that it is a skill that you already use. It is normal and effective. Many of us draw maps to help prepare us for a short trip across town. That is just a type of visualization that will help you complete your trip. Visualizing athletic ideas follows the same line of thought. If you can learn to visualize, you can: A) learn what to do in any given situation, B) respond immediately to practiced situations, and C) have less stress in your competition.

Skill building

Visualization can be used to learn skills, practice them, and to correct technique. This is accomplished by first practicing a skill, then learning to repeat the performance in your mind. Many gymnasts and divers can be seen using this technique when they are preparing to attempt a maneuver. Skiers in the Winter Olympics are often shown visualizing their runs before they began their competition. They mentally work on their performance before they actually ski down the trail.

This skill is not new to wrestling. At matches we see wrestlers "shadow wrestling" or going through a series of moves against an imaginary foe. Some athletes actually shoot a drop step across the mat and reach out, replicating a double leg attack. Others are seen hitting a high crotch on the invisible man. Sometimes the wrestlers' eyes are closed, other times they are open. Either way the athletes are so focused that they work with the thoughts that they are having and ignore outside distractions. The are physically practicing their skill while imagining a situation.

This type of visualization is a common and accepted practice in our sport, and it has several benefits that can be used by wrestlers. It allows the athletes to mentally practice their moves without having equipment or workout partners. It also gives injured athletes an activity that is sport specific. Some research suggests that athletes can develop improved reflex action and physical responses by including visualization in their practice routine. The tests show that our body actually jerks with the daydream, thereby causing the muscles to 'practice' as you think!

Stress reduction

Another use for visualization is in stress reduction or anxiety control. Theory says that if you can imagine yourself in a particular situation, then practice your reaction, you will be better able to handle that situation if it occurs. Most of us already do this. Practicing for a speech in front of the mirror or trying to guess which questions your teacher will ask on a test is an example of this type of visualization.

We often try to simulate specific events that we might actually encounter. This is not unusual, nor is it magic. Most of us have thought about what it would feel like to be champions or to win a big match. In guided visualization we just go one step farther. We understand that we are imagining a scene for a specific purpose, and then we try to actively direct or control the action that we are "experiencing" in our thoughts. By imagining stress-producing scenes, then finding solutions to the stress, we inoculate ourselves against that situation.

Two view points

Visions can be experienced from two points of view, and neither is right or wrong. One is an outside view. It is like watching a movie in which you see yourself as the star. The other is an inside view, as if you were watching from within your body. You can see the activity and feel the action, but you don't see yourself.

There is some discussion on whether one type is more effective than the other. I can find no proof that supports either as better. When working with athletes, I let them decide which they prefer. It might be more effective to use the outside view for imagining moves. You could see your positions better. I sometimes suggest that the athletes use an inside view for anxiety reduction. Some athletes seem to be able to "feel" the situation that way. I encourage the person to envision the setting, feel the situation, then focus on controlling any unwanted emotion that presents itself during the exercise. They should plan their reactions to the events, so if the athletes encounter these situations again, they will have already successfully dealt with the problems.

How to visualize

There are several different ways to envision a scene or match. Some coaches and athletes like to use a progressive relaxation script to relax and prepare the body. They try to get into the "mood" by going through a series of muscle relaxation drills. This approach helps some athletes, but I don't feel that the relaxation drills are needed. After all, most of us can shift into a good daydream without a formal preparation. (Remember when you daydreamed in that boring class?) Envisioning athletic scenes is much like enjoying a daydream.

You will need to get comfortable, then close your eyes. Try to see yourself in any setting. Don't worry about what you see. If you don't experience much success at first, just relax and try again later. Visualization is a blend of all of the senses, and it often takes time to learn. Remember, mental skills are just like our physical skills, and they will improve with practice.

Start with simple scenes, then progress to more complicated ones. You may want to add motion to your thoughts by going through abbreviated moves or actions while visualizing. Imagine exploding into your opponent or lifting him. Let your body lean, jerk, or twitch along with the thoughts. If you begin to sense the excitement and hear the crowds while you watch yourself perform, you are there!

Simulation

After you have developed your visualization skills you can become very selective in your thinking. Many athletes learn to visualize themselves in a specific gym, wrestling against a recognizable opponent. We call this practice *simulation*--when you envision a specific situation that you know will occur. You decide how specific it is and direct yourself through the process.

Want some examples? I knew a college wrestler who kept a picture of his rival on the wall so that he could use it to help get him ready to visualize. He would look at the picture, then begin seeing himself wrestling against the man in the picture. In another example of simulation, national television reported that the University of Alabama football team practiced for their Tennessee game while listening to Tennessee's fight song blaring away on stereo speakers. Alabama wanted to simulate the noise that they would be experiencing in the 90,000 seat Knoxville stadium!

Some of these ideas appear to be more than just visualizing or seeing. That is true. The more efficient you become in your visualization skills, the more senses you use. People who use the skill a lot report seeing, hearing, feeling, almost being in the vision. They become part of the process, like in a dream.

More common than you think

If you can't produce a brilliant masterpiece of a vision, don't fret. Any amount of success will heighten your focus, help lower your anxiety, and contribute to your overall performances. If you think about it, we all learn how to wrestle by using visualization and imagination. How so, you ask? Most of us learn by being told, "If he does this, then you do that", or "When you see this opening, shoot this move." or, "In this situation, do this." We are asked to imagine certain future situations, we practice to respond to those situations, and then we are expected to react to them as we did 'in practice'.

Isn't that also how we use visualization? Sure it is! We imagine future situations, we practice responding to them, then we hope to react to them as we did in our practice. Visualization is really a skill that we already know and use.

So, next time you have a spare moment but no workout partner to crush or throw, enjoy a self-produced mental movie. It could be fun. After all, <u>you</u> are the star of the show and <u>you</u> control the script!

Coach Hendrix takes his team through a group relaxation and visualization activity after practice. The athletes enjoy the activity and it allows them to reduce bodily stress and clear their minds of worry. By using guided visualization, the athletes can often inoculate themselves against future stress.

Photo courtesy of Cartersville Daily Tribune

Chapter 7

Hendrix uses mind over matter techniques for wrestlers

by Stephanie Ramage, Cartersville Daily Tribune

Focus: Does visualization and relaxation work with real athletes? What happens? How do they feel? What do they do?

Editor's note:

Mental skills are being promoted as assets to wrestlers, coaches, and teams. We hear a lot about mental skills theory and planning, but we see very little written on the actual application of these programs. How can wrestlers and coaches actually use these mental skills to help their performance? If you are interested in that question, you will surely want to read this piece.

For years, Coach Beasey Hendrix has offered Wrestling USA *readers suggestions on mental skills. We know you wanted to know if he follows his own advice. This article on Coach Hendrix's mental skills approach ran in the January 17th, 1994, Cartersville, Georgia* Daily Tribune. *A special thanks to reporter Stephanie Ramage, and* The Daily Tribune *for permission to run this reprint.*

About 30 sweaty young male bodies are sprawled on the floor of the Cartersville Wrestling Pavilion. A man in striped slacks is stepping over and around their feet and droning, "You like pink. Pink is a color you feel comfortable with..."

Oh, yeah! Since when is pink the color of choice among high school wrestlers? Since Assistant Coach

Beasey Hendrix came to Cartersville.

Hendrix is a strong believer in a mind over matter wrestling program that incorporates relaxation techniques like the one he was walking the guys through on a recent evening. He begins by asking them to close their eyes and tense up each muscle in their bodies, then to sequentially relax those same muscle groups. He tells them they are going up some stairs and then into a, well, quite frankly, a pink room.

Although this particular exercise is a group activity for any wrestlers who want to stay after practice and let their stressed-out bodies relax, Hendrix also works one-on-one.

After the other wrestlers leave, two stay behind. Matt Selman, a two time state runner-up, and Jeremy Knight. Hendrix ushers them into the weight room, away from the noise being generated by two guys farther down in the gym trying out their moves, and tells them to stand side by side.

He asks them what seems to be the problem and Selman tells him he is getting too wound up before the matches. He's worried.

"Usually I just think, 'Well, I'll do this and then this,'" but lately I've been thinking 'I've GOT to do this or I'm going to be in trouble,'" Selman says.

Knight says he's just really fatigued. He feels extremely drained after the matches and he can't sleep well the night before.

"What do you want then?" Hendrix asks.

"I want to be able to go through the match and do everything clean, the way I usually do," Selman said.

"Okay, so you want to visualize?" Hendrix asks.

"Yeah."

He asks them to close their eyes and then he tells Selman he will feel relaxed and fall forward. Selman, amazingly, almost like a zombie, does exactly that. He simply falls forward. Hendrix lightly touches his shoulders to keep him from falling face-down on the floor, then he makes the same request of Knight.

"Put your hands straight out in front," Hendrix

commands. "You will feel very relaxed."

"I am going to tie a helium ballon on your left hand, Matt, and I'm going to put a book in your right hand."

He pantomimes the actions and Selman's left hand mysteriously rises as if being dragged lightly up by a ballon. His left hand drops a little.

Knight goes through the same mechanics.

"Okay, we are going to go up some stairs and into the gym floor. It's time for you to go out to the mat. Coach (Chad) Phillips pats you on the back and you go. You take you stance, get ready, then shoot a single leg. It is a takedown for Cartersville. Two points. The crowd goes crazy. Coach Phillips says, 'Let 'em up.? So, you do. It's the second period..."

Yet another period is quickly dispensed with in the boys' heads. Takedown after takedown and the match is won.

"When we look good, we feel good. We have no fear. The ref slaps the mat. You've won. You have had a good meet. We have the best technique around and we enjoy taking people down," Hendrix says and a minute later he releases Selman and Knight from their trances, admonishing them to go home and enjoy some good food and relax with their friends and families.

In the semi-dark of the weightroom, it all looked like some hoodo-voodo, but Selman and Knight are quick to extol the virtues of Hendrix' techniques.

"I think it helps me a lot because it makes a big difference if you are relaxed and confident with your moves. Frustration can play a big part in not hitting every move smoothly," Selman added.

He adds that he can actually see every move when Hendrix walks him through visualization. He can actually see where his hands will be.

Knight agrees and says the technique helps him get focused on the match at hand, and it helps in another important area as well: it helps him in cutting weight.

"In the past, Matt and I would have to wear bags and tons of clothing and starve ourselves. But Coach Hendrix teaches us to take just small portions of food and cut down on the grease and think about how good that food is and how it is nourishing your body. You really don't have to eat much," Knight says.

Knight says his own problem is with fluids. He gets really thirsty, so Hendrix told him to suck on ice cubes and just concentrate on how much water his body is getting from each ice cube and how it quenches his thirst.

Knight weighs from 155-165 during football season, but he drops to a lean 145 for wrestling.

"People think football's hard, but wrestling is really harder," Knight says.

Hendrix knows that. In a sheaf of articles and papers he has written on relaxation techniques--he shys away from the word "hypnotism"--Hendrix carefully demonstrates the difficulties wrestlers face as compared to other athletes.

In addition to the fear of personal injury inherent to such a close combat-type sport, wrestlers have to deal with the isolation of being alone on the mat against opponents, because they can't fall back on teammates the way football players do. Add to that the constant pressures of weight control and you have the formula for blow-ups on and off the mat. That's why a good dose of sports psychology is so important.

Hendrix has an Education Specialist degree and a Masters degree in psychology from West Georgia College, and a communications degree from the University of Alabama.

Anything that helps them to feel more relaxed and more confident out there helps," Hendrix said. Before coming to Cartersville, he coached at Troup County for 10 years, and the team lost only 3 matches.

Chad Phillips, who is the head coach for the Cartersville wrestling team, says Hendrix has a different ideology, but they have the same goal. "I basically believe that if you get the physical stuff down, the rest will fall into place. My philosophy is that we can outwork people," Phillips said. "But, he had the wrestlers for about three weeks while I was still tied up with football and I came in and watched him doing relaxation one day. I saw 50 kids lying there with their hands kind of going up and I thought 'This has some validity'."

Phillips says that he believes it may be more effective on an individual basis than with a group.

Cartersville already has an 8-1 record for the year. Last year they were 11-3. In the meantime they are thinking pink.

Chapter 8

Using Relaxation and Visualization for Performances

Focus: Four All-Americans give examples of the different types of mental techniques that can be used to relax and visualize.

Mental skills play an important role in wrestling. We all know that. Athletes must control their mental processes to be able to compete at an optimum level. But, what mental skills can we employ that will help reach this "optimum level"? The intelligent use of relaxation and visualization skills can help wrestlers gain greater control over their thinking and can assist them in focusing on appropriate tasks while ignoring unneeded input. Let's take a look at these skills and how they can be used to assist athletes in improving their performances.

Four All-Americans

We often hear about mental skills training, but we never get the whole story. Most articles are presented in a vague manner, and no specific examples are given. What do coaches and athletes really do? What are these skills? How can coaches or wrestlers use them?

I have been fortunate in working with 4 Georgia wrestlers who gained All-American honors for the 1994 year. These athletes learned to use mental skills to enhance their performances. Each athlete used a different technique and each enjoyed different results.

These All-Americans have agreed to share the methods they used. This took courage. It is hard to open ones thinking for public inspection, but these four successful wrestlers wanted to help show that mental skills are a part of athletics that everyone, even World Champions and All-Americans, needs to understand.

Different skills, different needs

Relaxation is an important mental skill. It is the process of removing stress by thinking calming thoughts while overstimulating (flexing) the muscles of the body. Relaxation can be used in several situations. By teaming relaxation with visualization, many athletes are able to surpass the level of preparation they could achieve by using relaxation alone, or without using the skills.

1) Relaxation can help control activation. Wrestlers often become over-activated (too nervous), and their performances suffer. By using relaxation skills, athletes can learn to control their levels of activation.

2) We can use relaxation to work with negative self-talk. There are many areas of concern that can disrupt an athlete's focus. Weight cutting, performance uncertainties, and thoughts of injury can cause an athlete to engage in negative thinking. This type of thinking leads to tension which can negatively affect performances. By pairing relaxation with positive suggestions, we can help athletes overcome these negative thoughts.

3) Relaxation can be used to assist an athlete with visualization. The calmness achieved by relaxation helps to heighten the athletes' focus and allows them to concentrate on their visualization skills.

4) Finally, we can use relaxation paired with visualization to recover from matches and to conserve energy between matches. When wrestlers have a series of matches, they must be able to recover from each match, and then they must prepare for upcoming contests. By developing a specific system for recovery and energy conservation, athletes can recover faster and be prepared to compete in a more rested, less "banged-up" state of mind.

Mental skills for everyone?

The most common line of thinking probably says, "I thought only losers needed mental skills!" That's not the case! Actually, sport psychology techniques are important for all athletes. All levels of athletes, even elite athletes, can benefit from these techniques.

Sport psychology is a misunderstood discipline. Many people believe that it is an area of study filled with psychologists wearing horn-rimmed glasses, speaking psycho-babble! Fortunately, it is not. Sport psychology is simply the study of how athletes think while playing, practicing, or focusing on athletic concerns. Its techniques are most often used by coaches and athletes, not by psychologists.

It is hard for some of us to relate to the idea of using mental skills. A common belief is: if an athlete wants performance help, they must be crazy. Rest assured, neither of these All-American athletes were "crazy", nor were they "losers". They accumulated a glamorous 496-41 high school record during their combined 16 years of varsity wrestling. Their examples are of four (4) common situations that wrestlers can encounter. Their short case studies describe mental skills that can be used by almost everyone to assist with match preparation.

Relaxation for stress control

Matt (*Wrestling USA* All-American) often felt nervous before a match. He would notice physical stress such as a tight stomach, which in turn caused him to start having negative thoughts. This is common among athletes; physical tension is noticed, which causes negative concerns to appear.

Matt says, "I would feel butterflies and would start worrying. I would think about how much I didn't want to lose instead of thinking about what I needed to do to win. I had twice been in the state championship match, but lost both. This made me concentrate on what my opponent was going to do. Instead of being aggressive, I would become defensive."

Control your body

Matt learned to control his physical nervousness by using *progressive relaxation*. Progressive relaxation is where an athlete learns to tightly flex a muscle, hold it for a few seconds, and then relax the muscles. By overloading the muscle with a flex, the body tries to recover and rest when the muscle is relaxed. This leads to a feeling of relaxation.

We practiced the skill several times after wrestling practice, with Matt and another athlete being led through the steps of relaxation and visualization. Matt liked the control he gained over his body, and soon became so efficient in this skill that he would proceed on his own by using a relaxation tape.

"When I felt tension beginning to build, I would take the tape to a quiet place and simply listen to the suggestions. I would relax and ignore the feelings. It was great!"

How does this work? It is a simple approach. Since Matt felt that the physical tension triggered the worrying, he used relaxation to stop the body from becoming uptight. By stopping the physical symptoms, Matt would not begin the negative self-talk. That way he stayed focused on his technique and his plan of action.

Stopping negative thoughts

Travis, (USA Wrestling Freestyle All-American), encountered negative self-talk when he cut weight. Many wrestlers experience this, so it is a common complaint.

Travis says, "I became obsessed with things. My diet would be going okay, but I would start thinking about food. I didn't need to eat, I had just finished a meal, but I focused on eating all of the time. It would hit me when I watched TV, and even when I was driving my car. This really bothered me."

This seems like the same situation that Matt encountered, but it is actually the opposite. (Matt's physical sensations caused his negative thoughts.) Travis felt that his negative thoughts caused him to become physically stressed. This demands a different approach.

Travis had used progressive relaxation with a previous coach, so he was experienced with the technique. We decided to take that a step farther by using imagery to promote a change in his negative thought patterns. Travis used his relaxation routine to set the stage. First, he flexed and relaxed his way into a calm state of mind. This allowed Travis to center his focus. Then we discussed Travis' concerns, and some of the things he could do to attack these concerns.

How does this work? When athletes are relaxed, they enter into a highly focused state. They can concentrate on one topic while having very little outside interference. Experts say that this resembles, or actually is, a light level of hypnosis, and that many athletes will be open to suggestions in this state. So this is a good time to explain or discuss various topics with them.

Say what?

Travis was given suggestions while in this relaxed state. He would then repeat the suggestions by actually demonstrating what was said. An exchange might go something like: "Travis, when you begin to worry, sweep the worry right out of your mind. Notice the worry, then sweep it out." Travis would sweep a make-believe broom. "Take the negative thoughts about your match, ball them up, put them in a bag, then throw them away. You don't need them, so throw away your bad thoughts." Travis would grab the thoughts, ball them up, then throw them away in an imaginary trashcan. By "pairing" the idea of removing the negative thoughts with a motion or activity, Travis was encouraged to recognize and "remove" his negative thinking.

"At first I thought it was weird. It was strange. I could hear everything that was going on, but I didn't seem to care about anything except listening. I would do what I was told, then forget about it. But, it seemed to work."

"I soon noticed that the eating thing wasn't bothering me anymore. I didn't constantly think about food. When I did think about food, I would just eat lightly instead of gorging. I would take a bite of tuna or something and then stop thinking about it. The mental training helped me control my thinking," says Travis.

Enhancing visualization

Josh (*Wrestling USA* All-American) liked to spend a moment resting and gathering his thoughts after practice. He enjoyed the basic relaxation method and quickly mastered its steps.

"I liked to lie on the mat and do the relaxation. We would watch ourselves shooting takedowns and would try to relax. I always felt better after we did it," he said.

Josh wanted help with his offense. He had an excellent stance and good defensive skills, but he had trouble scoring. This centered around being a heavyweight. As a heavy, he was worried about making a bad move, then getting caught under his opponent's weight.

Since Josh was experienced with visualization, we decided to use it to encourage him to develop an offensive series. He was lead through several visualization sessions where he learned to relax, then envision himself successfully scoring on an opponent.

Seeing is believing

"I would see myself turning the corner, either ducking or finishing my Russian 2 on 1," said Josh. "I could first see myself doing it. Then I got where I could see myself while I was practicing. I finally got where I would see myself go all the way through the move, finishing with a full back arch. A 5 point touche fall!"

Sometimes, Josh would picture himself against an upcoming opponent that he knew would be tough. (We call this "simulating" a performance.) By "wrestling" an opponent in advance, Josh was able to remove the anxiety that would normally be present at a match. He felt like he had already been there.

Josh neutralized his concern for "getting caught" by visualizing (and practicing) a side attack. He soon perfected a duckunder and arm drag series, and thereby avoided shooting underneath his foe. By pairing his visual images with his physical practice, Josh was able to develop a takedown series that he felt comfortable in performing. By seeing himself being successful, he developed confidence. This confidence allowed him to try a series that complimented his physical attributes and lessened his previous concerns.

Recovery and conservation

Sean, (Junior World Champion), knows that it is important to be ready for each match. But at the 1994 USA Junior Nationals, he also learned that recovery and energy conservation can assist a wrestler in preparing for matches.

A returning dual national champ, Sean faced the challenge of having to wrestle several times a session for a number of days. He was entered in both styles-- freestyle and Greco-Roman, thereby, facing the possibility of wrestling nearly 20 matches during the week. A nagging injury also entered the picture, so we wanted to do everything possible to assist this athlete in being at an optimum level for the tournament. What could be done to help him meet the demands of a week of competition? Are there any mental skills that can be used to help athletes get through the physical and mental challenges of a long week of high level competition?

Overlooked skills

Recovery becomes very important for the elite athletes. In tournaments, the less skilled athletes are put out in early rounds, but the elite athletes stay in the event for many rounds. (At the USA Junior Nationals, wrestlers usually have to fight at least 6 bouts just to make it to the round robin, and each match is against a progressively better opponent.) This causes these athletes to accumulative bruises and bangs as the tournament continues. It, therefore, is a necessity to address this wear and tear.

Conservation of energy is also important. That is the idea that you <u>can not</u> stay "pumped up" for extended periods of time without negatively affecting your performances. You must learn to bounce your emotions--get ready for your match, perform, then calm down and conserve energy until your next bout.

Sean says, "Often I would watch other wrestlers. I would get into their matches and then start thinking about mine. I would get a 'pre-pump' of adrenalin, and that would make me nervous. I would have to walk around to calm myself. I had to think about other things, or I would actually get mentally ready for my match way too early. Then I would feel drained by the time my it finally came."

This too, is a common problem. Many things can cause athletes to become prematurely excited. This activates their nervous system and can actually "burn them out" <u>before</u> a match. What can be done to help athletes who experience this situation?

The process

The first step is to encourage the athlete to relax between matches. That is hard for many athletes to do. It sounds good--just relax, calm down, rest, and don't worry about it! But the emotional high of the last match and the uncertainties and excitement of the upcoming matches can leave an athlete in a naturally activated, or nervous state.

I begin teaching athletes this skill by discussing "recovery". A wrestler's body goes through a battle. To recover, the athlete needs to relieve the pains and to regain strength. Then when it is time for his next match, he can arouse himself to the proper level of readiness.

With an athlete

Sean reported to our training room after his first session. We discussed his post-match condition; we evaluated his physical condition and state of mind. Relaxation, paired with massage, was used to allow Sean to fully relax. This was a support group situation--

several wrestlers exchanged massages, then were taken through a guided relaxation session.

After the wrestlers relaxed, we used visualization to enhance the recovery. They scanned their body for tightness or sore spots. Each athlete focused on his specific needs.

Sean was told to see himself grow smaller--so small that he could fit on the head of a pin--then even smaller. He was to see himself perfect in every way, just "very small". He then "watched" himself enter a tiny capsule which was placed into his body. This new, "small Sean" would travel throughout his body and massage the aching areas from with-in. That would be easy since "small Sean" knew where all of these areas were.

"I saw myself in a little spaceship. I would go to the sore areas of my body, get out, take my hammer and beat the dents out. I have to laugh when I talk about it now. I realized how funny it sounded when I was telling a teammate about how I recover. But, hey, it works!" says Hage.

After Sean learned the recovery skills, we discussed the idea of relaxing between rounds to conserve energy. We reviewed the benefits of "bouncing"--get ready, compete, recover, relax, then get ready again. The success with the recovery reinforced the ideas of conservation. Sean felt comfortable resting between sessions. He began to use the relaxation and visualization skills to his advantage. Our only fear was that he might become **too relaxed** and not ready for his next match. The staff monitored the situation closely, but were happy to find that this concern was unfounded. Sean has developed an excellent prematch ritual that includes an activation process which insures that he will be ready for each match.

Sean says, "I used to look at the whole tournament, trying to figure out who would do what. I would get excited and stay that way all day long. Then I would feel drained. I realized that I only needed to focus on who I had for the next round and not worry about everybody else. I guess I tried to fight the whole war at once. Now I just plan each battle, one at a time, and I prepare for that battle. I relax and stay focused instead of thinking about all of the other stuff that is going on."

Skill mastery

So, each athlete learned to use a mental skill that addressed a specific area of their competitive life. By employing these techniques, they enjoyed the results and they learned that knowing mental skills can be just as important as knowing a counter to a move.

Learning the skills was easy. All of the work was done in the open, with other wrestlers joining in or watching. Each skill had certain concepts that had to be mastered before the next step could be carried out. Once mastered, the skills became a part of the athlete's way of doing things. After a little practice, each athlete was able to continue his technique with-out outside help, and the skills became a part of that wrestler's way of preparing for competition.

But...

There may be a little reluctance to use the skills. Many people don't feel comfortable working with this area of sport. Some coaches and parents feel that psychological methods "mess with the athletes' minds". There are others who believe that it is against some religions to use these methods.

I have had little trouble with my athletes using these skills. We are very open with what we are doing. I make sure to use skills that are promoted by "experts", and our national organizations. I keep copies of articles that explain the techniques, and I educate the athletes and parents as to what is going on. If questions arise, I explain what we are doing and show how it is an extension of what the wrestlers are already doing in everyday life. The major concern appears to be that parents are not familiar with the techniques. Questions such as, "What if they don't wake up?" "Will it make them crazy?" "Does this open them up to be possessed by the devil?" do occasionally come up. We always respect the feelings of the athletes and their parents. No one is forced to take part in the mental skills programs, so any athlete may opt out of these activities.

So...

Using relaxation and visualization can be an interesting and valuable adventure. It will be beneficial for all coaches and athletes to investigate the skills and to see where they could apply these methods to their programs.

There may be some uneasiness felt with the first couple of attempts at relaxation or visualization, but these skills will improve with practice. Soon you will be wondering what took you so long to add these exciting and performance enhancing tools to your wrestling toolbox!

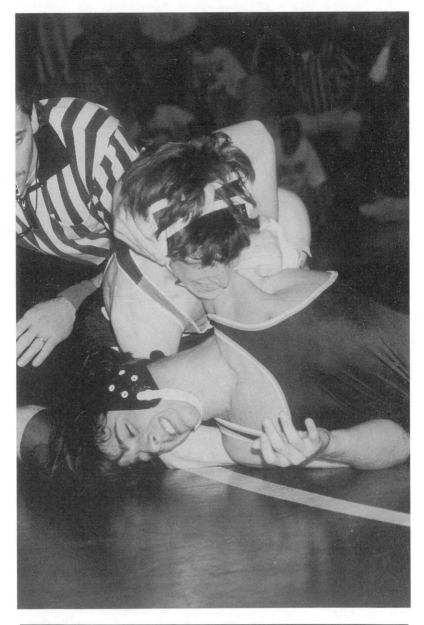

Will you be ready to compete? How will you handle the ebb and flow of your match? How do you prepare for a match. Do you have any special strategies?

Photo courtesy of Wrestling USA

The match is the culmination of our many efforts, and it tends to be the testing grounds for judging how we are doing in the sport. Are you ready for the test? Here 1995 Greco World Champion Dennis Hall shows his emotion after another one of his big victories.

Photo courtesy of USA Wrestling

Section II

The Match

Articles
 9 **Preparing For A Match**
10 **Start The Match**
11 **Recover**
12 **Reframing**
13 **Critic Or Coach**
14 **Top, Bottom, Neutral, or Defer**
15 **Win Or Lose**

Top level performances are not accidental. They result from a mixture of ability, preparation, performance, environmental input, opponents, and luck. To enhance performances, wrestlers can use an organized approach to prepare long-term and at the match to be ready.

They can be taught to handle problems that may occur, and can also learn to have a specific mind-set that will help their performances. Athletes can start preparing for a match by looking at the progression of a long preparation. Focus then shifts to the actual match.

Events or situations may arise that can cast negative effects over the match. Wrestlers must learn to recover from unfortunate happenings and to control what they can. Thinking styles can affect the way an athlete looks at something, as can the way a coach works with an athlete during a match.

Finally, the wrestler will benefit from understanding some of the strategies behind what position to choose when he is asked that familiar, "Top, bottom, neutral, or defer?"

Chapter 9

Preparing: Looking at the Total Picture

%%%

Focus: Preparation is more than just warming up. An organized approach, starting days before the match can be beneficial.

%%%

The match is the moment of truth, and an athlete must be ready, both physically and mentally, for a top level performance to occur. Hours of hard work and practice boil down to a short six minutes of competition for high schools, and five minutes for international.

But just how do we prepare to wrestle? When does the preparation actually begin? What really needs to be done? These are good questions that that should be addressed by all athletes and coaches.

The fox and the boar

A fox was walking through the forest when he ran into a wild boar who was sharpening his tusks upon a tree trunk. "Boar," said the fox, "why are you wasting your time sharpening those sabers? I don't see any hunters, and there are no enemies in the area. Couldn't you be doing something a little more important or worthwhile? You should probably be putting your time to better use."

"Fox," said the boar, "you are not as heavy a thinker as you believe yourself to be. You have no understanding of the real world. For, you see, if I must fight for my life, I'll have no time to sharpen my skills; I will have to engage in the attack. So, it is best to prepare before the need arises, as you see me now doing."

"Oh," said the fox, embarrassed that he had not known such a logical thought, and had been corrected by a lowly boar!

Preparation

Prepare, you say? Yes, prepare we must, because "preparation makes perfect"! We all understand the need for physical practice and conditioning. Our sport is based upon the idea of physical combat, so those two areas of expertise are a basic requirement. But there is much more to being ready to fight than just knowing your moves and being in shape. There are other areas in which we should prepare that will allow us to reach a level of peak performance.

Total picture

Psychology has a branch called Gestalt. In simplest terms, Gestalt is the study of the total picture versus its parts. In wrestling we are all aware of the physical requirements, but often we do not look at the total picture. We fail to concentrate on other important concepts that contribute to our performances. Often, we fail to look at the total picture until something has gone wrong or has caused a problem.

If we looked at the Gestalt, or total picture of wrestling, we would see the area of physical training, which includes conditioning and moves, but we would also see an area covering mental preparation. This mental portion would have several sectors. We could look at the point of performance (when you are actually at the meet), the day of the competition, the week of the event, or maybe even longer preparation. We could also look at topics such as strategies, stress control, diet, activation, self-talk, and even goal setting.

But, that is a lot to think about, and it makes preparation for a match appear complicated and involved. Is it that involved? And if it is, just how does a coach or athlete prepare for all of these things? The best way is to plan and organize your approach.

Plan and organize

As we have seen, there are several things we can think about when it comes to preparing for your match. If not handled properly, any one of these topics could cause problems with your performance. The key is to organize and plan a system that is optimum for you. Consider what you need, what you like, and what is best for you , and then follow through on the plan. Learn to stay away from negative influences. Focus on completing activities that are beneficial to you, and then stay with your plan.

Three phases of preparation

A checklist approach to preparing for a match or weekend event may be your best bet. Break the program into three phases: 1) build-up, 2) point of performance, and 3) competitive phase. Each phase has a specific place in your mental skills program, and each can affect the level of your performance. Let's take a look into the different phases so that we can get an overall feeling for each.

1) Build-up-- The build-up phase is the base or foundation for a good competition. It includes any activities that relate to your competition for the day or two before your event. Think of it as setting the table. This is the time when you begin to narrow your focus from general life events to your competition. During this time you should try to plan activities around your schedule for performing. You can't control everything, but you can get as much as possible in order. Aspects of this phase include: Last work-outs before the meet. What to eat? How much sleep or rest? What social activities? What to think about? How much stretching? What equipment or uniforms do you need to pack? And any other concerns that may affect your preparation.

2) Point of performance-- When the athletes reach the gym, they have different needs. Time management becomes a major concern. When do you perform? How much warmup do you need? Water or not? What type of activation or stress control do you need? How is your

self-talk? What is your focus? What are your game plans? Do you have your 'stuff' ready? Is your support group working?

As you move closer to competition, activation and stress control become more important. Even things that appear to be minor can affect your performance if they are not taken care of. Examples of point of performance problems that occur frequently are: A) when a wrestler fails to warm-up properly and enters the match cold or not activated. B) negative focus causes an athlete to engage in inappropriate self-talk or worry.

3) Competition-- When your name is called, it is SHOWTIME. Your thinking needs to shift from focusing on preparation, to actually performing. Strategies and self-talk become important. Training and mental skills blend together to push you through your performance. You compete, and then receive feedback.

Sound like a lot? You might think so at first, but successful athletes have always used this system. It is nothing new. We are just identifying and organizing a system that you can actually use to do to compete successfully.

So, now you should be ready to take a look into <u>your own</u> system of preparation. Fill in the blanks, apply your needs to the following outline, and customize it to fit your personality. Then use the results to help prepare you for the big meets or tournaments that are headed your way!

Your preparation checklist
Build-up skills

1)   Eating--What type of meals do you like to eat? How will you make weight? What will you eat the day before? The morning of? Is there anything you need to stay away from?

2)   How much of a work-out do you need the day before? How much stretching? Do you need to run or walk the night before? How much exercise the morning of competition?

3)   What is your best rest or sleep schedule?

4)   When do you organize your travel bag? What do

you need to include?

    5)   What do you want to think about? Any visualization? Relaxation?

    6)   What types of social activities? Time alone? Someone to talk to?

Point of performance

    1)   What environment do you want in the stands? Away from the crowds? With the team? What setting is best for you?

    2)   How much warm-up? How much water?

    3)   What is your focus? Music? Rest? Relaxation?

    4)   How do you control your activation and stress?

    5)   What type of self-talk do you want to use?

    6)   Do you make a plan? An alternate plan (Plan B)?

    7)   What do you need from your support group? Reminders? Left alone? Cheers?

Competition

    1)   What do you think about right before you compete?

    2)   Is your strategy planned for the match? Plan B?

    3)   What is your activation level? Need adjusting?

    4)   Did you visualize?

    5)   Scan your body. Make any needed adjustments. Perform to your best level.

How to prepare

So, how do you organize this total package of preparation? There are several things you can do.

A)   Athletes can learn to control what they do. You can't control the environment, but you can control your approach to performance. The greater the number of things that you have organized, the closer you are to removing uncertainties that may cause stress.

B)   Set a schedule. By knowing what you want to do, you remove questions that can affect your anxiety level. Develop an approach that covers these questions.

C)   Plan how to keep your schedule. Make alternate

plans that can be used if a problem arises. Look at a worst case scenario, and make a list of possible events. Be ready to handle each situation, much like you practice to counter certain moves.

D) Ritualize. Develop a system or routine that is comfortable to you. Repeat it so much that it becomes automatic. Dress in the same order. Have a set prematch meal. Listen to the same music. Go to bed at the same time. Get a routine that is yours.

E) Coaches can assist athletes by:

1) allowing the athletes to have input into some decisions, and including them in the plans.

2) teaching them how to prepare mentally.

3) encourage the athletes to take control of their preparation and responsibility for being ready.

But beware!

Becoming so structured can be a two sided sword. A team or athlete can become obsessed with a program. It can be hard to adjust if an unexpected problem breaks the flow of your routine.

Need an example? Okay, let's say that you really believe in your lucky socks. They have become part of your prematch ritual. You want them, count on them for luck, and believe that you need them. What happens if you forget them? Do you panic? Forfeit? Perform poorly? No, you just have to go on with the rest of your plan. Unfortunately, we can let outside events become so important that they produce stress when they really have nothing to do with the meet. So be careful that you don't place so much importance on your preparation that it overshadows the match.

Seek solutions to problems; focus on the solution, not the problem. Learn to adjust. If things don't go exactly right, then welcome to the real world! We try to set things up so that they are optimum, but problems do occur. You must learn to recover, and then redirect your focus, or work to overcome the unexpected obstacles.

Conclusion

Understand that the way to reach peak performance is to have things ready so that you are comfortable with yourself, your plans, and the environment. Be prepared <u>before</u> the match. Things will be more comfortable if you remove as many of the uncertainties as possible and just get into your game or match.

Have your plan organized and systematic. Know what you are going to do and when you are going to do things. Have your schedule planned and your things ready. Predict problems that might occur and have "Plan B" already drawn. When you recognize a problem, shift your focus to finding a solution.

<u>You</u> hold the key to <u>your</u> preparation because <u>you</u> are the only one who really knows what you want and what you need. So, like the boar in our story, take a moment to sit down and prepare for that upcoming battle. Organize a system that will allow you to be ready to wrestle. When you hear your name called, it's SHOWTIME, and all of the preparation must come together to allow you to perform at your optimum or best level.

If you can reach the point where everything goes so smoothly that you don't have any worries or concerns, then you have made it. Your efforts should be directed at becoming almost automatic in your performances and responses to predictable situations.

Chapter 10

Starting the Match "Focus on Success"

Focus: Matches can be won or loss because of prematch preparation. What should a wrestler do to be ready? What are some of the problems wrestlers face? Are there solutions?

You've warmed up. The weight class before you has just finished and it's time for you to do your thing. You walk to the mat, step on, and head to the center circle. You are now ready to wrestle.

Or are you?

Preparing for competition can be a complicated task. Athletes must take care to be ready, both physically and mentally. Coaches usually do a good job of teaching their athletes how to warm-up physically. Wrestlers are taught to stretch, jump rope, exercise, and shadow wrestle until they feel loose and break a sweat. We see this at matches, as most wrestlers are aware of this concept and are encouraged to be ready to compete.

But what about getting ready mentally? How many coaches teach this subject? What do they teach? Is there a system that can be used to help students learn to prepare mentally for a match or competition? These are good questions that probably need some discussion.

Preparation at the match

Getting ready mentally can be a challenge. Thousands of thoughts can run through an athlete's mind right before a match begins. You might think, "He's pretty big, and he's got a good record," or, "I saw him wrestle and he had a tough headlock". Your coach may even tell you to stay away from his upper body. So, what do you do?

Successful wrestlers enter the match knowing what they will be trying. They direct their thinking to what they can control. A major problem is that some wrestlers focus on what their opponent can do. They think, "He's a thrower." Coach even says not to tie up with him. That sounds good, but what are you going to do? If you choose not to tie up with him, where does that leave you? What if he tries to tie up? All you have really planned is to avoid his tactics. By avoiding his style, you focus on what not to do and that doesn't help you score points!

Wrestlers need to work on stating their goals in a positive, task-based form, directing them toward what to do. Instead of thinking; "He's a thrower. Don't tie up", restate the thought as; "I want to drop my levels and attack his legs. My single is my best leg attack. Let's see what he can do when I shoot inside and control that leg."

If your man is a leg rider, you might think "I don't want to let him get his legs on me. He's good at riding and turning." This type of negative statement will not help you perform. It will only cause you to focus on his attempts. How can you restate your plans in a positive form? You may want to concentrate on your takedowns. Say, "I'm going to show that big-headed, smart-aleck a real takedown clinic. On my feet, takedown, release, takedown. He'll get dizzy just trying to add up the score. Touch, drop my level, then high crotch. Bang, bang, bang, 6-2 lead. He's a dead man!"

Problems with focus

Major problems can arise. One problem is focusing on things you can't control. This often shows itself when the wrestler begins to think, "What if he does this, or what if he does that?" We can't control what our opponent is going to do; we can only control our actions. It is okay to develop a plan of action for situations that might occur, but we can become lost anticipating our opponent's actions. So, develop your plan based upon what you like to do, then make a "plan B" to use if "plan A" hits a snag.

An example? As a heavyweight, I like to make contact, then pummel for my arm drag series. That is my plan A. But what if my foe won't tie-up or he begins to fake toward my legs? I drop my level, and then I begin my shuck and snap series, redirecting his motion. I refuse to play a game of chase--I'm not quick enough. I don't panic; I just realize I must make him fight my type of battle. *Now, I am using my plan B.*

Another problem wrestlers experience is focusing on things that don't matter. We often hear athletes talking about who their opponent has beaten, or which team he is from. That shouldn't matter. If you begin to focus on those facts, you will lose touch with your plans and begin to think too much about changing your style. Some athletes focus on their opponent so much that they freeze up and have trouble completing their moves.

It is good to scout, but use the information to make plans that will assist you in performing. I always like to know an opponent's tendencies. This allows me to develop a plan that I can use to attack. But I try to make sure to design my plan around what I can do and what I can control. If he is a leg attacker, then I must do something that brings him up to my upper body. If he doesn't like to make contact, then I have to be patient, keep a good stance and force him to make contact.

Practicing your focus

Control your focus when you are drilling. In the practice room, think positive, goal-oriented thoughts before you begin your flurries. Look at your workout partner as a foe. What do you want to do? How can you get it done? What does he do well? How can you make him fight your style of battle?

Make a plan, and then see if you can follow it. Try to manipulate your partner into stepping or moving where you want him to go. If he tries a move, focus your attention on what you need to do to score. Stop thinking about what he is doing, and begin to focus on your plan.

Once you begin to think this way, you will see your

foe in a different light. He becomes something that you are trying to manipulate instead of something that has control over you.

A coach can do several things to help you focus. At practice he may discuss how to plan a series, and then how to set it up. He can give you some suggestions on what to do. At a match he may ask you what you want to do, trying to get you to focus on your first move. His job should be to get you to move away from the negative thoughts and help you move toward thoughts which will lead to success.

Remember, the key suggestions are:

1) Plan your match around what you can do and what you can control, and practice using this approach.

2) Have your coach help you before the match by asking you what you want to do.

3) Tell him in a positive, goal-oriented statement what your plans are, and explain to him what you are going to do to beat your foe.

Closing

So next time you get ready to walk on the mat and shake hands, be ready both physically and mentally. Plan your first moves and a general strategy for the competition. Be ready to do your thing and make the match flow in your direction. This won't guarantee success, but it will give you a goal or direction from which to begin.

Don't plan your match around avoiding his moves. Instead, plan your match around performing things that you can do successfully. Choose a strategy that promotes your strength, yet minimizes the strength of your opponent. Stay away from negative thoughts. By telling yourself what <u>not to do</u>, you make yourself become cautious and inactive.

Work to attack his weaknesses with your best moves. Each time you go back to the center, have a move in mind. Be ready, and explode into your plan. After all, making him fight your style of match is much better than you trying to stay away from his techniques.

Are you ready when you step on the mat? Coach Steve Day of Team Georgia helps All-American JW Dukes prepare for a match in the Junior Nationals at Fargo North Dakota.

Ready to Wrestle?

1. Be physically prepared by warming up.
2. Have your first series or set-up in mind.
3. Focus on what you can do, not what he does.
4. If your foe does something well, focus on how you can effectively attack him.
5. Use positive and task-based thinking. Make statements that say <u>what you are going to do</u>. Stay away from thinking about what you are not going to do.
6. If you recognize negative thoughts, redirect yourself towards accomplishing your goals.
7. After flurries or changes in situations, return to the present. Think about what you need to do <u>right now</u>!
8. Take charge and have a good time!

Chapter 11

Recover!

Focus: Problems will occur. How can we handle them? What are some of the strategies that can be used to overcome these problems?

The match is going well. You have a four point lead, time is running out, and it looks like you have it made. Just hold on, run out the clock, and coast for the last 30 seconds.

Then, wham! Out of nowhere it strikes! So sudden, so smooth, that you don't even know what happened. But you feel it. You're on your back and in danger. Now, what do you do?

Wrestling offers us a chance to win or lose at the drop of a hat. Two seconds. That's all it takes. From a big lead to sudden death; it is part of the game. Pinned. Stuck. Caught. Decked. Flattened. Smashed. These are all terms that describe that sudden moment of misfortune.

This is a common situation in our sport, and unfortunately, it can place us in a frustrating and dangerous position. So just how should a wrestler handle this type of situation? What should he do when he suddenly finds himself going from being in total control to having to recover to win?

The Cat and the Fox

There once was a young kitten. She was walking in the back of the pasture when she spied her friend, the fox. Fox walked up to her and said, "Howdy, kitty. What's cooking?"

Kitten didn't really like the fox's attitude, but she wanted to talk, so she played along, and sat down for a nice conversation. They spoke for a while about the weather and local news.

Fox heard, off in the distance, a pack of hounds baying at some unknown victim. This started him bragging about all of the techniques he possessed that allowed him to constantly escape from harm. "I can run in a small hole if need be, or I can do long distance sprints if that is what I want. I can hide in the deep grass, or run along a fence, or cross a creek. Whew, there's just so much I can do," he beamed.

Cat shook her head and said that she had only one way to escape. "I must climb a tree and sit it out, awaiting the pursuer to tire, grow impatient, and leave," she said.

"Wow," said Fox. "That ain't nothing. You need to learn more so you can be in control of your destiny," Fox added, showing his know-it-all attitude.

About that time a group of beagles topped the hill. Cat reacted immediately, jumping straight up onto a tall oak tree that was nearby. "Hurry, Fox," Cat meowed as she climbed toward the highest branches.

Fox looked around, trying to decide which way to escape. He didn't know what to do. He was confused by the noise and became uncertain of which way to run. "Why me?" he said. "I knew those dogs where on the other side of the farm. Blast, how did I let them sneak up on us? It just can't be!" he added. Fox went blank, and then panicked. He looked for a hole, and then he tried to find a fence line. Finally he attempted to outrun the pack. Unfortunately, his delay allowed the dogs to cut off all possibilities of escape. Surrounded, he had to surrender to the baying hounds.

Cat was horrified at the outcome. She sat for a minute. Then she thought, "Fox claimed to have many avenues of escape. But you know what? When a problem occurred, he got so confused and uptight. He couldn't figure out what to do. I think it's probably better to know one safe, sure way, than a hundred proposed avenues!"

Losing control

Getting tossed, being reversed, suffering through a

bad call, an injury, or even attempting a bad technique can cause sudden shifts, not only in the momentum of the match, but also in the wrestler's thinking. We often see the wrestler argue with the referee, hit the mat in anger, panic, freeze, or just give up. It's not surprising. A wrestler can get confused, lost, or angry when he encounters a problem. He doesn't know what to do, so he pauses, thereby allowing the opponent to take control of the match. That pause, that hesitation, that moment, could be the difference between being a champion or being an "also ran". Like Fox found out: ***He who hesitates is lost!***

So, what should a wrestler think when he realizes that he has run into trouble? Kitty had some good advice that we can use in the wrestling circle. It is important to learn to quickly use that one technique you need to escape a dangerous situation. Getting angry, questioning fate, or getting stressed will not help. You must learn to recognize the danger and then react quickly, performing a move or technique that will allow you to immediately recover from the situation.

The trained athlete realizes the dilemma and immediately attempts to counter or correct the problem. Unfortunately, many athletes are not able to make this quick adjustment. When something bad happens they pull a fox and get so confused that they don't know what to do.

What is going through their minds? Some are shocked. They think, "What happened? Where am I? What did I do?" They are actually lost. Some start to go through denial. You will hear them say, "No!" as they refuse to admit their new situation. Others may panic, going into an uncontrolled frenzy or maybe even go blank on the mat, allowing their opponent to take total control.

These are normal human reactions that are documented by psychological research. People will react in these ways when confronted by a sudden, threatening situation. Unfortunately, these types of reactions are often the ones that get us eaten by the dogs!

Actions to take

So, what does an athlete need to do? You have to recover and realize where you are. It doesn't really matter what happened. It just happened, and your first reaction should be to quickly recover to a safe position, stabilize the situation, and then work to regain control.

1)   Learn to recognize when you get into trouble. That is not as easy as it seems. Because of that denial, shock, or panic, we often are in a haze when it comes time to recover.

2)   Accept the fact that you are in trouble. There is no time to question how or why it happened. You can analyze that later when you talk with your coaches or watch your films.

3)   React. You must keep moving and work to complete a move that will take you to safety or put you back into the match.

How do you <u>train</u> yourself to recover? It is important to drill this concept in the practice room. Set aside some time in the practice schedule to drill the technique. Drill specific situations so that you can get the feel of what happens. Practice recovering from getting thrown. Learn to become aware of your body position and react. Get that 'feel' of what to do.

Memorize the term *"recover"*. Have your coach or team members say the word while you are on your back. Train yourself to realize the word recover means: "Oops. I'm in trouble. What do I need to be doing right now to get back in control? I need to..." After you learn to think that way it will become almost automatic.

You can also practice your self-talk. While practicing your bridge you can actually talk yourself through the action. Think, "I'm on my back! Bridge and turn. Fight. Get out of bounds!" "I'm on my back! Bridge and turn. Get out of bounds!" "I'm on my back. Bridge and turn."

If you are on your back, you must fight your way off by using sound techniques. There is not much time for thinking--just go right into your bridge series. You can: 1) Slide your hand between you and your opponent, and then quickly turn your belly and body to the mat. 2) Try to complete a high bridge, rolling your foe. 3) If you find yourself near the edge, then get out of bounds.

There are other situations that might cause problems. One might be that last second takedown that puts your opponent ahead. What do you do? Just give up? No, you begin to hit your switch, sit out, stand up, or roll as soon as you can gain body awareness. You may even be able to hit a move before you settle to the mat.

Simulating these situations is a good way to learn how to recover. You can practice late match takedowns by having your partner shoot a takedown. As you fall to the mat, think of a way you can immediately reverse or escape. Don't wait until you hit and settle down. Learn to pop that falling switch, wing roll, or standup so quickly that your foe doesn't even get control.

Coach can help by including sudden misfortunes in the practice session. He may want to make a bad call, or give out the wrong score in a scrimmage. How will the athletes respond to these types of sudden unexpected problems? Do they recover their focus and work on continuing their match, or do they dwell on the problem so much that it disrupts their performance?

Conclusion

The bomb can drop anytime, and he who hesitates is lost. Learn to immediately go into a recovery phase every time you encounter a sudden shift in a match. Bring yourself into the present. Think, "What do I need to do?" Then focus on solutions. Solve the problems by quickly going into action.

You can practice your recovery techniques. Simulating specific situations is a good method. Include being thrown, losing the lead late in the match, suffering from bad calls, or even errors in scoring.

By learning to overcome these sudden shifts in momentum, you will be better able to bounce back. By having the presence of mind to fight your way through these challenging situations, you will become a tough competitor; you will be one who will always be a threat to fight to the very end!

Chapter 12

Labeling, Framing and Reframing

Focus: Wrestlers think during a match. The way they think about situations can actually affect their performances. How does the way you perceive something affect the way you react? Can you change?

The offensive wrestler shoots in for a single leg. The defensive man limps a leg, swivels his hips, reaches for a whizzer, and then settles to the mat. The battle has begun. What comes next? That's a good question.

The answer to this question depends on the thinking process of each athlete. That's because the way the athletes think and feel about the situation will affect their performances. The course of action taken will correspond to how each wrestler "sees" or "labels" the situation. If the athlete perceives himself in a favorable position with a chance to improve, he will fight. If he sees himself in a position of little or no hope, he will let go and give up the points.

Framing

Athletes learn to recognize situations, label them, then to respond to the label that they apply to those circumstances. To develop these labels, they use a mixture of experience, formal learning and instinct.

An example of labeling or framing would be: your opponent drops his level, attacks low, and wraps his arms around both of your legs, his head on the outside. You immediately label that a 'double leg' and think,

"Counter the double. Legs back, hips in hard, dig my crossface. Redirect his penetration. Butt drag." An experienced wrestler doesn't take much time to recognize this, but beginning wrestlers may have a long lapse between the initial attack and an appropriate response. Often, because of an inability to recognize or label what is occurring, a young athlete can't call upon appropriate counters. The beginner must be coached into responding.

Experienced athletes are able to frame the situation into a big picture, comparing it with similar situations they have encountered. The labels they use come from the results of how different actions or moves worked in these similar situations. This is then filed in their memory. Therefore the ability to call upon appropriate reactions and to respond quickly comes from being able to recognize the situations and to remember successes or failures that have resulted from previous attempts in those situations.

We call this label making process *framing*: putting things in an order so that they form a total picture or way of looking at something. The way we frame things is based upon many factors, but is greatly influenced by how we think.

More on framing

Being able to recognize a situation and frame it in an appropriate light is very beneficial for the wrestler. Poor labeling of predicaments can result in poor decision-making; therefore, performances are hampered. Anyone who has ever encountered his first *guillotine* can attest to this fact. You didn't really recognize that your opponent had you in a cross-body until you reached back and grabbed his head. Heck, you saw it there and thought you could pull him on over. Unfortunately, he pulled your arm through, shot his half, and locked in for a painful near-fall or pin!

You did not identify the situation as a cross-body ride, so you placed yourself in danger by reaching back. Hopefully, next time, you will recognize the situation, correctly label it, and then try not to grab that head!

Reframe

Reframing is the skill of looking at a circumstance or situation from another point of view; this helps you to view things differently. It is like thinking about something in another way or seeing it in a different light.

Reframing can have a definite positive outcome on your thinking and performing. It is most commonly used to combat negative thinking, and it can help you to look for alternate solutions to newly redefined problems. There are some tricks in learning to reframe a thought. First, you'll want to focus on what you think you will "need" to do. Just what do you want to accomplish? What are your goals? Then you will have to work to reach those goals.

Coaches can help athletes learn to reframe by presenting a problem as a search for a solution. Teach your athletes to reframe the situation from a problem into an opportunity. Make it a challenge rather than a dilemma. Teach the wrestlers to focus on what they can do to see the situation from a different angle. There are many ways to label things or to think about things, and the athlete's way may not be the best way. Actually, the athlete's way of looking at something may be part of the problem.

Example of the concept

Many coaches teach a defensive maneuver called the sprawl. Most of us know it. This is the technique of the defensive man throwing his feet and legs back, dropping his hips, and trying to make room between himself and the attacking wrester. It is most commonly used against the leg attacks.

Coaches who teach this technique train their wrestlers to recognize and respond whenever their foe begins to attack the legs. The athletes use the sprawl as a counter move by jumping back and placing their weight on the head, back, or shoulders of the aggressive wrestler. The athletes are taught to think, "He's attacking my legs. Get back. Sprawl." The athletes are instructed to react immediately to avoid the attack. They listen to the coach give those instructions, and they practice and drill the sprawling to ingrain this concept into their defensive system. Thereafter, whenever an opponent attacks their legs, they recognize this as a danger; then they jump back into the sprawl technique.

Trash that one

I threw that term out long ago and reframed my athletes' concept of defending against leg attacks. We decided to attack our foe when he tried to get into our legs. Now, an opponent's leg attack is no longer a danger. It's been reframed into a chance for us to score.

Why did we change this? Because we had a totally defensive frame of mind about being attacked. My athletes could get their body back and were reasonably successful at stopping their opponent's attacks, but we had trouble scoring from the sprawl position. (Doesn't everyone?)

I kept seeing a position where I thought we could score. Many of our opposition's shots were not picture perfect. They lacked in technique and force. They weren't penetrating; many just flopped into a half-hearted attack. But my wrestlers would sprawl back, and pop back up into their stance, ready for the next flurry. If only we would stay in there and fight instead of taking ourselves out of the battle by sprawling; I knew we could take advantage of the poor techniques being shown by our foes.

Solving the problem

The solution was that we needed to *relabel the situation*; we needed to *reframe our thoughts* about the matter. Instead of thinking, "He has shot at my legs, I need to get back", we needed to think, "Okay, he is out of position. He is too low. Now I can put weight on him, cross face him, smash him with my hips, and turn the corner or butt drag. I'll score on him from here."

Our coaching staff began to use that train of thought in the practice room, and in match situations. When we saw a wrestler begin a leg attack on our athlete, we immediately began to encourage an offensive attempt. Instead of yelling, "Get back! Sprawl!" we would reframe our man's line of thinking by saying, "He's out of position. Punish him. Turn that corner. Score from there." We practiced the situations in the practice room and verbally reinforced the idea. Our athletes learned to drop their level, cross face, grab an ankle, and then turn a corner.

We actually began to have the athletes repeat the phrase, "He is out of position, punish him. Score by freezing him and turning the corner." Pretty soon our athletes began to think that they could score, that they were suppose to attack in that situation instead of just trying to back out. They successfully reframed the concept. Now instead of fearing an opponent's single or double leg attack, we looked at it as a chance to get them out of position and for us to score.

Accepting the concept

"It takes a while to get accustomed to the idea," says Coach Dariel Daniel, 1993 NHSACA Wrestling Coach of the Year. "We get so used to playing it safe. We often encourage wrestlers to focus on not being scored upon, to sprawl or avoid contact. This keeps the matches close, but in the long run it hurts our sport by making the matches boring. Score once, hold on and win--that is the strategy that many people are now using, especially in championship level matches.

"By reframing the sprawl situation we encourage the athletes to score. We open up the match, add excitement, and also teach our athletes to take advantage of a mismatch. The athletes now recognize that their opponent has left his safe stance and is extended. If we can tilt his balance or disorient his shot in any way, we have taken a strength position where we are at an advantage. We used to waste this advantage by sprawling because we saw it as a situation where our opponent was being aggressive. Now we try to key upon it and score. The situation is still the same as it was, we have just *relabeled* or *reframed* it for the athletes.

Recognize and label

Let's look back to our lead paragraph. The offensive man shot and grabbed a leg. The defensive man limped, hooked a whizzer, but was then knocked to the mat. If defense thinks, "He's got my leg. I'm off balance and I'm in trouble." He will probably look to bailing-out, turning towards the mat and giving up the takedown.

If he thinks, "His weight is too low, off his base. I need to do this to score. I'll try to get my hips back and clear my leg," then he will begin to move toward solving the problem. He may try to scoot his hips out, plant a foot, throw a whizzer, stand back up, throw his foe's head out of the middle or do a dozen other effective moves. It all depends on how he has been coached, how he labels his situation, and what counters or moves he knows.

Helping wrestlers reframe

There are several ways wrestlers can be helped. The most basic way is to teach them to see any situation as an opportunity to use several options. The next way is to offer the athletes many solutions; teach them several ways to react in the different situations that may arise. The more ways they know, the more ways they can label or frame a situation or predicament.

Increased confidence is also beneficial. As the athletes build confidence, they will think of ways to solve their problems or to improve upon their positions. This often comes from experience (especially successful ones).

We can help build this experience by simulating different situations in practice and giving the athletes verbal cues to assist them in labeling what is happening. Explain to the athletes what they can do. Teach the situation from several view points. Teach the athletes there are several different ways they could be looking at the situation.

Example

Over the last couple of years we have had several matches come down to the heavyweight battle. In a few of them, our big guy, Butter, had to pin for us to win-- twice in the county championships alone! As an underclassman, Butter felt a lot of pressure. He had never faced this type of situation, so he wanted to talk before his first "had to pin" match began. "What should I do?" he asked. "I have got to pin him or we will lose," he said with a little nervousness in his voice.

I knew this athlete's attitude. He was a talker and a showman. He liked to be in front of the crowd. What could I do to shift or reframe his thinking away from the the "I gotta" approach to a way of thinking that would enhance his performance? I chose to focus Butter on the limelight, to point out how he was "fixin" to be the hero. "You'll look good tossing him," I offered, before Butter stepped around the bench. "It'll be great being the hero. Everyone will cheer and think you are Superman," I added.

"Yep," he grinned as he stepped out on the mat. "I think I'll like that," he quipped back. A handshake, a series of pummels, then a crashing underarm spin to a fall gave us the county crown! Butter had reframed his way of looking at things, and it helped him relax and perform.

Other situations

There are many situations that can be reframed to help athletes increase their chances for having good performances. Wrestling a returning champion might be thought of as a hopeless exercise by some athletes, but you may be able to <u>reframe that</u> into a chance to score a big upset. Wrestling in front of a big crowd could be seen as a scary event that shakes up some athletes. Reframe that into a chance to let a lot of people see your great technique.

A common problem we see with wrestlers is a great amount of negative self-talk which is really framing a situation in a negative light by looking at the bad that may occur. Often we can improve performances by having the athlete <u>reframe their outlook</u>. What good things might happen? What does the athlete want to happen? What positive opportunities does the situation offer?

It can be the same with almost any idea. We often hear our athletes talk about leg riders, upper body experts, or rollers. When athletes begins to put labels on the expected outcome of their matches, often it becomes a self-fulfilling prophecy. They focus so much on the label they can't think of what they are suppose to be doing. That's why it becomes very important to help athletes supply the right labels. If the label or frame does not help the athletes in their approach to their situation, then they should reframe that picture in a different light.

Closing

So, basically, framing is the mental technique of labeling or recognizing something according to your system of thinking. Reframing is the skill of renaming or relabeling a situation so that one sees the situation from another angle or point of view; one looks for a solution or advantage instead of the problem. It is a beneficial skill that is often used by those optimistic individuals who seem to accomplish so much.

Is your glass half empty or half full? Do you attack or sprawl when he shoots a double leg on you? What would you think if you were Butter and had to pin for your team to win? Only you know the answers, but if you are a competitive wrestler, you will surely want to be able to see the situations from every angle and develop an appropriate course of action.

Now it's time for you to reframe or relabel. Look at things from a different viewpoint. Think about situations in a way that will assist you or your wrestlers in seeing the positive results that might occur if only you look for solutions instead of focusing on the problem.

Chapter 13

Critic
or
Coach?

Focus: The wrestler made a mistake. How should this be handled by the coach? What is the best approach for correcting mistakes or making adjustments during a match?

The flurry just ended. Your athlete planted a foot, exploded up, and tried to complete a standup. To your dismay, he forgot to gain hand control. The opponent grabbed a tight waist, blocked your wrestler's heel, and then drove him to the mat, out of bounds. Your athlete is lost and confused. This is the third time he has failed to complete his standup, and he doesn't understand why.

You are furious. You have spent hours of practice time working on hand control. What is he doing? What is he thinking? Why is he not hand fighting?

As he returns to the center of the mat, he looks to you for advice. It's late in the match, and the score's tied. What should he do? What should you say to him? How will you say it?

Will you be a *critic* or a *coach?* Coaches are often placed in this position. The athlete misses a point of technique that has been worked on for uncountable moments in the practice room. It looks so simple to us, the athlete should just do what he is taught. But he's not performing. What is wrong with him? Why won't he finish the move?

It's frustrating. Anger swells up inside. You want to fuss. You want to scream. You want to get him moving. As a matter of fact, you want to do anything that will get your athlete back into the match!

But, what can you do or say that will help him get back into the flow of the match and overcome that lost or confused feeling? Let's look at what coaches can do by first looking into an old tale that may address the issue.

The coach, the boy, and the river

There once was a young boy who was playing near a swollen river. His coach came by and saw him nearing the water.

"Step back from there, Sonny. I don't want you to fall in and get swept away," the concerned old coach said. "You could get killed," he added with an understanding smile.

The youngster nodded his agreement, then stepped back. When the old coach turned his head and began to walk away, the athlete ran back up to the edge of the water. Unfortunately, the boy slipped on a wet rock and fell head over heels into the swollen and raging river. The current swept him away.

"Help! Help!" cried the athlete. "I said help!" he screamed as he thrashed about in the churning water.

The coach looked over and became disgusted. Running up to the water's edge he said, "If I told you once, I told you a 1000 times, stay away from the water. Now look at you! You are in the water being swept away. Didn't I tell you to be careful? What am I going to do now?"

Coach took a long breath and began again. "Didn't I tell you to keep your rear-end away from there?" he asked. "I knew you were going to slip into that water. I just knew it!" he muttered. "I should have..."

"Yes! yes! yes! yes! yes!" cried the boy. "I know what you said and I should have listened, but please, HELP ME NOW! Fuss at me later!"

Using the concept

Just like the boy in the story suggests, when you find your athlete in need of help, do just that--offer him simple directions or calm words of encouragement. It is best to direct the athlete toward completing a move. Give positive suggestions that address some technique or strategy. He may be lost or confused, not knowing the score, time remaining, or even what position to choose. He may even be frustrated with himself, knowing that he is making good effort in trying a move, yet failing to successfully complete it.

"Good job, Billy. Good standup. Remember your hand control. Get hand control as you come up," might be a way to redirect his focus. In another situation you may wish to say something like, "You are two points behind. Let's get that reversal. Hit your switch." That will help bring your athlete back into the present. By using positive talk and then giving a positive, task-based directive, you assist your wrestler in finding a solution. You encourage him to develop a goal that can help him overcome his opponent.

"Dead gum it! What are you doing? You will never get free like that. You are wrestling stupid!" might be the method chosen by some coaches. But if you choose to question his intelligence or criticize his attempts, you will actually cause him to focus on the problem. You may focus him on an area of confusion and failure. Like the boy in the river, your man needs your help, not your anger.

So when you find yourself in this type of situation, think about the type of assistance your athlete needs. If he needs help in selecting top, bottom, neutral, or to defer, tell what to do. If he is not penetrating, tell him to "penetrate, shoot through the man". Dropping a head on bottom? Tell him to "keep your head up", then suggest a move to complete. Work to get him back into his match by giving positive instructions that he can quickly understand.

You may even want to develop a set of hand signals to use in case you are on another mat, the crowd is cheering loudly, or you are afraid that your opponent might be listening.

You only have a few seconds to communicate. That's just time enough for a quick thought. Don't waste time with complicated instructions, and don't make him focus on useless questions or angry comments.

Conclusion

So anytime there is a break in action, whether the period has ended, the wrestlers go out of bounds, there's a penalty, a stalling call, or even an injury, have your athletes to look your way for help. But stay away from those emotional lectures, criticisms, or questions. There is just not enough time for a sermon, debate, or long answer. You'll have to give that short, sweet kernel of advice that will bring him back into the fight.

Remember your wrestler's cry of, "Please, <u>HELP ME NOW</u>! Fuss at me later." Give your athlete a suggestion that refocuses his thinking towards performing winning techniques. You can always talk about other things after the match when the excitement and tension has lessened, and you have the time to engage in an open and meaningful discussion. It will surely help your wrestler's performance and maybe even lower your blood pressure!

Chapter 14

"Top, Bottom, Neutral or Defer?" What'll You Say?

Focus: How do you choose your starting position for the second or third period? What are the strategies behind making that choice?

You are in the midst of a battle. Your foe is a skilled wrestler and is giving you all you want. If you can only get through this period and win the toss, you know you can take control.

The period finally ends. The referee looks your way and asks that simple question-- "Top, bottom, neutral or defer?" What do you say?

If the match makes it to the second period, someone will be asked to choose the starting position for that period, and then again for the third. Just how does one make that selection? What criteria should one use to make that choice? Is there some strategy behind choosing your position?

You bet!

There are ideas and strategies that will help a wrestler make a wise choice when it comes to starting positions for a new period. These choices are not easy--a lot depends upon situations that are occurring on the mat, your personal style, and your team's philosophy. And there are probably no right or wrong choices, just situations that require you to take a "best possible" position. So, let's take a look at some strategies behind choosing a position to start the second or third period.

Your strength

The first consideration should be your personal style and strengths. This will be based upon your best style, or where you are the most comfortable and confident. Where are you the best: top, bottom, or on your feet?

Many wrestlers have total confidence in their particular skills and have no problem making the choice. If they have set a record for most takedowns in a season, they will probably choose neutral. If they have the best cradle in the world, top. If their switch is a killer, then they will probably choose bottom. That makes sense. You want to go with your style and make your opponent fight your match.

I had a friend in college who was average on his feet, but if you ever let him on top, so long, he cradled you to death. We just hoped he would make it through the first period, then win the toss! There was no doubt what he was going to choose, and he was successful with this strategy.

Momentum

Another concept that should be considered is the momentum of the match. Are you killing him? Have you turned him twice in the last 30 seconds. Has he ridden you to death? Has either of you been dominant on your feet?

You will want to continue the momentum if it is going in your direction. If your opponent has momentum, you will want to change the flow by choosing the position that stops or reverses his attack.

Dariel Daniel (Troup High School, La Grange, GA) says, "If I have seen a definite mismatch in one of the areas, say I have 3 takedowns and he has none, or I have turned him twice in the first period, I will want to keep that going. The takedown man would choose neutral, the turner would choose top."

Score

What is the score? This is especially important in the third period. Is the match tied? Can you score from bottom? With the score tied or within one point, many people choose bottom in the third period. They feel that they can escape, and tie or go ahead. This is an effective strategy, especially in high school where there is no riding time.

Most athletes feel that they can get up from bottom, but there are a couple of thoughts that you might want to consider before you make this choice automatically. One, has your foe been successful in riding you in the previous periods? Is he a leg rider? Have you been able to control him on the mat? How did you do while you were on your feet? What kind of shape are you in? How about him?

Because of our focus on takedowns, if it is close, our athletes usually choose neutral, but if you feel you have a great chance to escape and make it close, tie, or take the lead, then do it! Choose bottom. You have to do what you have confidence in performing. After all, you are the one who has to perform and do the hard work.

Strategy

Sometimes there is a special strategy that you may want to follow. Are you in good shape? Better than your foe? You might want to base your choice upon a strategy that involves who is in the best shape. If your opponent is not in shape or you want to focus on a perceived weakness, you may choose your starting position to attack that area.

We used to wrestle against an athlete who was tough in the first period, so-so in the second, and horrible in the third. You can bet we circled and pummelled in the first, chose top in the second, and tried to wear him down, then just did what we had to in the third. He was usually so tired by then that it didn't matter.

Coach's observations

Your coach may see something that moves him to help you make a decision. He is watching and analyzing the situation. He is removed from the emotion and has a good idea of what is happening. Several times I have had our heavyweight choose top, although he was actually better on his feet. I noticed that the officials were allowing our opponent to back out, neutralizing our offensive abilities. We decided the best situation would be to attack him on the mat.

Ron Gray coach of West Des Moines' Dowling High School (Iowa State Champions 1990-93), says, "I try to evaluate the flow of the match, then balance that with my athlete's ability level and style. I want him to look my way at the break and I will offer him a suggestion based upon what I have seen."

Defer

The strategy to defer is one that brings the most debate. Some coaches feel that it is best to take charge of a match and choose your best position. Others take a more cautious attitude and, like the football coach, defer to the next period.

My feelings are based upon the idea that if we are doing what we are supposed to, we may never see our opponent's best series because we can tech him or get a fall. I rarely ever ask my athletes to defer. Why give him a chance to dominate? So, unless there is an overwhelming reason, we will always take our choice based upon what we feel will best serve our purpose.

Beware

Often we see a wrestler take his man down, then turn him several times. The successful wrestler may even secure several takedowns. He definitely shows superiority on his feet and on top, yet, when given a choice, he chooses the only position that gives his opponent a chance--bottom. This is the one area that we do not know of our opponent's ability. What if he is a leg rider, or has a terrific top series?

In this situation, there is no logical reason to choose bottom! This may be the only situation where he can beat you.

What if he took us down, we reversed, then we turned him twice. You can bet my man would choose top. Yet, I have seen wrestlers in this situation choose neutral! That's the only area where their opponent has scored.

We often have to snicker at our opponents when they make a choice. At Cartersville, we tend to be good at takedowns. During the 1994-95 season, our team had almost 900 takedowns in varsity competition. We may have 4 in the first period. If we can't break down or turn our foe fairly quickly, we will cut them loose and try for a new takedown. Our opponents see us let people go. This makes them think bottom is a good choice because they will get a point.

But is it? What if we already have 3 takedowns on you? If you get an escape, we are probably going to take you down again. What could you do on top? We don't know, and we don't want to know! We will gladly give you a point to keep you from choosing top, especially if we have been taking you down at will.

Simulate decision making

We practice making choices at practice. We cover the team's strategy and explain why we are doing each selection. It is hard for younger athletes to understand these guidelines, but with a little discussion and practice, they soon learn to make a preliminary choice, then look for the coach's suggestion.

We may stop the practice and ask an athlete, "What would you choose?" He then must tell us what he would choose and why. Then we vote and have a discussion.

Closing

There are no absolute right choices, only selections that are based on momentum, skills, situations, and mathematical odds. And these are open to debate. You must be able to apply these loose ideas to your personal style, match situation, and coach's philosophy.

One thing is for certain: You must make sure that you plan for situations in advance. Know when you would like to choose one position or the other. The referee will only give you a couple of seconds to make the call. Look quickly to your coach, get his input then make your decision. Your strength, match momentum, score, your strategy or your coach's observation can give you a hint.

You may not agree with the reasons or selections stated above. That's okay. By helping you think about your opinion we will assist you in developing a plan or set of criteria for you to use in your match. So, next time he looks your way and says, "Top, bottom, neutral or defer?" you will be ready with an intelligent and logical answer.

Top or bottom? Once the period starts it doesn't matter. The choice has been made and you must work hard. Here we see both wrestlers battling to overcome their opponent.

Photo courtesy of Wrestling USA

Chapter 15

Win or Lose: Evaluating performances

Focus: Did you win or lose? How did you do? What happened? Winning or losing is important, but the idea should not dominate our thinking.

The referee walks to the center of the mat. He takes the athletes by the hand and shows the crowd the winner. A raising of the hand symbolizes the victory. One head is held high, eyes gazing proudly through the crowd. The other head faces the ground, gaze dropping toward the mat. It happens in every match and is part of our sport's ritual.

In the wrestling world there are no ties. We will have a winner and a loser in every match. Someone will be champion, and the other will be the defeated warrior. From a performance standpoint, just what does that mean? How does winning and losing affect the way we look at our performance?

Do you fall into the trap of evaluating performances based upon the results of winning or losing? If you do, don't feel alone. Many coaches, athletes, and fans do. But, if we aren't supposed to focus on winning and losing, what should we look at? How do we know what to do after a match? What should we do?

Winner or loser?

Our society places a premium on winning. The words we use to describe successful people refer back to this fact. Winner, champion, can't be beat, he's the best; these are all labels that are used to denote people who are successful. Labels such as these are attached to people who perform well, who have achieved, or who have obtained success. These labels are positive in nature and are usually welcomed as descriptors by anyone fortunate enough to be called such names.

We also label or notice people who are not winners. Often we hear, "He's a loser, can't beat anyone, could not beat my grandma." "He's a pushover." "They're not tough." These labels are stuck on personalities who have not been successful. They are applied to people or athletes who are deemed unable to win. The names carry a concept of failure. No one wants to carry such a title, and youngsters often use these names as insults.

And that's not just on the mat. These ideas and names can be carried over into a wrestler's daily life. They can affect both his way of thinking and the way he feels about himself. As a matter of practice, these labels are even used to describe people who are not athletes, nor even in competitive situations. It seems that our society likes to use competitive terms to describe any success and failures.

More to it

Athletes and coaches need to overcome this temptation to evaluate or label based upon winning and losing. Performances should not be judged by win/loss records alone. Records are important, but we emphasise this concept too much. There is much more to evaluating a performance than just looking at the won and loss records. Records, scores, and other outcomes only focus on the last part of the match. They freeze the last second of the competition and fail to give feedback as to what occurred in the match. The score does not tell of actual battle, it only reveals who met the criteria for scoring the most points.

We must take care to look into other statistics and use other methods of evaluation if we want to understand how well we wrestled, or if we want to use our matches to improve our performances.

How well you perform

The key to understanding and enjoying a performance is in being able to evaluate how well you did. Were you good, bad, mediocre? Did you wrestle to your level? Above it? Well below? To do this, you must remove yourself from the emotions of the win/lose game. You must be able to step back and evaluate exactly how well you performed.

Look at the kids playing in the backyard. They keep score in an informal way. More often than not, they focus on playing and will change the scores or situations if it is necessary to keep the game going. It is not uncommon to see youngsters "make it more fair" by spotting the other team make-believe points, or giving an extra player.

Think back to your backyard days. Do you remember scores of your daily games? Probably not. But most athletes I speak with can tell me about the great plays that occurred in some of those games. (I remember one. Joe dove for a line drive in our "whuffle ball league". He caught it just on the tips of his fingers as he crashed into the bush by Mrs. Rankin's house. When he rolled out, we all cheered. To our amazement, Joe had a big yellow jacket hanging off the end of his nose. Without knowing it, he had landed in a yellow jacket's nest! Before we could yell, it popped him! He screamed and ran. We laughed and cried and ran after him, not knowing what to do. I don't remember the score, but I sure remember that play!)

Different situations

Some situations should make an athlete feel good about performance. They are the levels of performance we are trying to reach. These are levels where the athlete performed as well as he could. The performance matched the athletic skill level of the wrestler.

To win while playing well is the goal of any athlete. If we perform well and gain a victory, we tend to be happy. We have reached performance and result goals.

To lose while playing well is hard to take. We have

done a good job, but come up short. From a performance standpoint, this is acceptable. You did what you were trying to do. You just didn't score enough, or the other team was better. Remember, we can't control what others do. If you reached many of your performance goals, then you did what you could.

Overcoming adversity gives an athlete an extra good feeling. A bad call can make it tough. We can have bad luck. Illness or injury may show its ugly side. But when we are able to overcome these problems, we get a boost, an "I can beat the world" type of rush.

Other situations are not so positive. They usually cause a negative feeling to occur as we try to evaluate our performances. Winning while playing poorly is one such circumstance. We have won, but there can be an empty feeling. Questions as to why we didn't perform well begin to float into the minds of the more perceptive athletes. Others, who are not so aware, will just consider it another victory and will fail to use it as a yardstick that show they need improvement.

Losing by a bad break or bad call is another emotional setting. We often hear an athlete say, "I was robbed, cheated, had bad luck, had an unlucky break." In this type of situation, it can be hard to evaluate your play if the match was filled with unusual situations, bad calls, and bad luck.

Losing while wrestling poorly is another. This is usually the easiest situation to understand. When we know we did not perform well, we can accept the outcome. In this setting we must try to evaluate what happened. Why did we have a crummy match. Was it everyone, or just you? How can we recover and get back on track?

Problems

Our society places much of the pressure on the athlete. Pressure can appear to come from many places. Pressure can come from your school mates. They are constantly teasing and picking at you. Your coach may be one of those win-at-all-cost people. He might not be able to handle losing, and he may pass this unfortunate characteristic on to you. Your family is another place where you may find pressure. Finally, you, yourself may be guilty of building a wall or wave of emotion based upon winning or losing.

Judging self-worth based upon athletics is a very common problem among our society. Because of the aforementioned pressures, many athletes think they are no good if they lose. The opposite can also happen. Some athletes become self-centered and egocentric because of their successes on the mat. They feel that, because they are successful wrestlers, they are also successful people. Other athletes can suffer from low self esteem. Their record is not glamorous and they had some problems in winning. Because of the lack of a winning record, they begin to feel like they are not successful people.

The overall results of these pressures, the rewards to the winners, and the negative effects of losing, help to build and promote that win-at-all-cost attitude.

Solutions

Evaluate performance using realistic reviews based upon obtainable goals, and common sense. What did you want to do? (If you just said win, then turn to the goal-setting chapter and take a look at goals and goal- setting skills.) How many of your short term goals did you reach? Which ones did you not reach? What would you do differently to change the outcome if you could rewrestle the match?

By deciding what you would do differently, you are designing a plan to remediate any problems or errors.

Accept it. What happened did indeed happen. If there are things you can change, then get to work on changing or correcting. If you did all you could, and after taking a moment or two to analyze your performances you can not identify any problems, then ask someone you trust for their opinion.

We should not celebrate intensely nor mourn excessively. This may seem like an "old fogey" statement, but I really feel that we should put a little dignity back into athletics. Too often we see the winner start to jump up and down, turn to the opponents and taunt their crowd, or just act like a fool. A little emotion after a big win or upset is understandable, but unsportsmanlike actions take away from our game.

Many of you may have seen a youngster acting like his match was the world championship. I often have to tell my athletes to take it easy. I'll ask, "Is this the first match you ever won? You sure are acting like it."

It's the same with losing. Wrestling is such a personal sport. We often take the results and personalize them. We feel that the other team or athlete does not like us, or we began to act like we don't like our opponents. If we lose to someone, especially if it's a close match or we got a bad break, it is hard to control the emotions. Hour after hour of hard work has been put in the match. Athletes that are result-oriented think that they have now wasted those hours of preparation.

We can see the athlete lose control and begin to do things that are not socially acceptable. Screaming, hitting the wall or breaking windows, cursing out loudly, wandering in circles, or grabbing at their heads are just some of these behaviors. I was once in the unfortunate position of seeing an athlete punch the official after losing a close match on a referee's call.

These actions must be controlled. Win with humility, lose with dignity. That is the only way we can keep middle school, high school, and college athletics in the schools.

Conclusions

The thrill of competition revolves around the concepts of winning and losing. Unfortunately these ideas can interfere with a coach or athlete's evaluation of performances. The stereotypes of winner and loser can also follow an athlete off the mat. We must learn to judge our performances on more than the win/lose record.

Evaluate. Then use this information to adjust and improve.

We are not the results of our matches! We are complicated arrangements of physical, mental, emotional, and spiritual components. When sports take over someone's life, it is time to re-evaluate their motivations. Learn to wrestle, and enjoy it. It is usually not life and death!

Kurt Angle accepts congratulations from the table workers after winning his 1995 Freestyle World Championship in Atlanta, Georgia.

Photo by Doug Reese

Coach Ron Gray of Dowling High School in West Des Moines, Iowa, gives some encouragement to his athlete. Ron hopes his wisdom will help his wrestler in getting ready to wrestle.

Section III

Getting Ready
To Wrestle

Articles
16 **Look, Listen, Feel The Pressure**
17 **Drill If You Will**
18 **Hendrix Tridot System**
19 **Heat Is An Enemy**
20 **Obsession With Eating**
21 **Tennis Anyone?**

Learning to properly prepare for your matches will help your performance. Take a moment to look into some of the ideas behind practice and getting ready to perform.

Each wrestler has a specific method for learning. Many go through practice without thinking. You can help yourself learn. Start to look, listen and feel the pressure.

Why practice? Why drill? We need to understand drilling and repetition. We can incorporate special drills in our work-outs that will focus on specific techniques. The tridot drill will polish your cornering technique and will teach you to penetrate and get behind your foe.

Weight cutting is a common problem in our sport. It has several aspects that add negativism to wrestling. The obsession with eating, and the use of heat as an aid in cutting weight are two of these negative aspects.

Finally, we can use tennis ball drills to improve our stance and motion. By incorporating these simple ideas, you will improve your position and learn to penetrate deeply into your opponent's danger zone.

Chapter 16

Look, Listen, Feel the Pressure! Learn To Learn

~~~~~~

Focus: People are different. Some athletes like to talk, others like to watch, even others want to feel the action. What is your style?

~~~~~~

You walk into the practice room wanting to be a wrestler. You are ready to be a champion, but you need to know the moves and rules. Without this knowledge, you stand very little chance of accomplishing your goals. You want to get better, so what do you do? How can you get this knowledge? Just how does an athlete "learn" to do those neat and complicated takedowns, throws, and reversals?

Help yourself learn

There are several things you can do to help yourself absorb the important information that your coaches and workout partners are going to offer you. You can actually prepare yourself for learning.

"Prepare myself for learning?" you ask. Yep! It's really no big deal; you've been learning all of your life. Only now, you want to learn, so you have to think about learning, and like breathing, it seems harder to do when you think about the activity.

One thing that educational psychologists recommend is that you teach yourself how to learn. That sounds like a strange idea, but it's really not that hard. You can learn to learn! Let's look at some of the ideas behind learning, let you think about them, then hope they will become part of your practice system.

Focus

Focus means many things. In its broadest sense it means to narrow your concentration to a specific area or thing. Focus is the basic skill that you will need to bring into the practice room. You will be required to focus on several different things, and the major challenge will be in learning what to focus on.

This will depend on what your coach suggests, and what your strengths and strategies are. Your coach will develop a certain system which has an underlying philosophy or approach. Within his design will be a style that will be right for you. He will help you by directing your focus to specific moves and ideas that will be appropriate for your body style, skill level, experience, and maturity.

How to focus is another question. As we just mentioned, you are directed to focus or concentrate on certain areas by your coaches. Coach can point you in the right direction, but you must be the one that pays attention and absorbs the information. How you focus will have a lot to do with what type of learner you are. You will have certain learning styles that will dictate your learning approach. Let's look at the different types of ways we learn and see if we can design a method that will help you pick up more wrestling knowledge, thereby giving you a chance to become a better wrestler.

Learning styles

There are different styles of learning. Some athletes like to watch. We call them *visual learners*. Others like to use words. We label them *oral* or *auditory learners*. There is still a third type. They like to feel the move or action. We call these wrestlers *kinesthetic learners*.

How can this knowledge help you? If you are a <u>visual learner</u>, you need to place yourself where you can see. You need to be able to <u>watch the demonstrations</u>. Many people are visual learners. They like to see things and can actually get a better idea by observing a demonstration of an activity. As they see the action, their brain sorts through the information and stores it in a manner that allows them to remember and perform the activity. These athletes benefit by using videos and picture books to supplement their learning. So, if you are a visual learner, try to watch closely. Get the *picture*?

Other athletes are <u>oral learners</u>. They would rather <u>listen to the description</u>. If you think you are an oral learner, then you need to make sure that you get the key words that describe the action. To oral learners, words offer an added dimension to learning. Oral learners need to hear a description of the action so they should learn to focus on the voice of the presenter. *Hear* what I am saying?

<u>Kinesthetic learners</u> like to <u>feel the action</u>. They like to experience the feeling of what is going on. A kinesthetic wrestler would want to be the dummy, or demonstration partner. If this is not possible, then they should move their body along with any description or demonstration so that they feel the progression of the movement. It might be best to stand in the rear and mimic the technique being shown. How do you *feel* about this?

Thinking styles

There are also different types of thinkers and each type has a preferred style. Some like to see the whole move, then "tween" or fill in the middle parts. We call these students *global thinkers*. Others like to go step by step, wanting to perfect each task before moving on to the next. We call these people *analytical thinkers*.

Global thinkers look at the total movement. Knowing where something starts and finishes gives them a boundary in which to work. They can then fill in the middle parts with an uncanny sense. Global thinkers usually don't really need much specific teaching. They attempt to create a total movement that accomplishes the task. You often see them practicing complete moves from start to finish, as a whole. If a global learner develops a problem in style or an incorrect part of a move, it can be hard to fix because this athlete has problems understanding pieces of the whole.

Analytical thinkers like to know the parts of the movement. They like to understand every little movement, and why it was done. Analytical athletes to go through a step by step process of learning. They often practice moves by working on transitions from skill to skill. They may: drop their level and penetrate, drop and penetrate, drop and penetrate, then move to penetrate-lift, penetrate-lift in a progression, hardly ever shooting a complete move. These learners can get so involved with the parts of a move that they have problems learning to go through the complete motion.

What is your style?

Which style best describes you? That is something you will have to decide. It really doesn't matter which you are, but it does help for you to know your style. If you can decide which is your dominant learning and thinking styles, there are some things you can do to help yourself use your strongest style. You can attempt to place yourself in the most beneficial position for learning. You can also try to look at things from another style to complement your strength.

Hints

If you are a <u>visual learner</u>, *close your eyes and imagine yourself performing the move.* Visualize yourself in action. Try to see yourself completing the action. Take another view from a different angle. Watch the action or demonstration from this view.

If you are a <u>verbal or oral learner</u>, *tell yourself what you want to do.* Break it down into verbal bits. Remember the commands and words that describe what you are trying to do, and then actually think them to yourself. Make an oral outline. A duckunder would become: "Stance, penetrate, make a window, lower my level, turn the corner, knock 'em down or lift 'em."

<u>Kinesthetic learners</u> should work to *feel the pressures and movements.* Watch and listen, but apply the directions to the movements. Allow your body

to twitch and move as the coach demonstrates the moves. Volunteer to be the model or demonstration dummy. Shadow wrestle the move. Ask someone to show you the move by actively using you as their partner.

What's the best way?

As we have said, each athlete has a dominant style. It will be best to use that as your usual style. But you also need to use all three learning styles when possible. This will give you additional information that may help you experience the technique from a different point of view.

Learn to look, listen, and feel

1) Watch the coach or athlete demonstrate. Notice where they are and which way they move.

2) Listen to the instructions and comments. Repeat the key words or directions to yourself.

3) Physically practice the move from both offensive and defensive positions. This will give you a feel for what is taking place.

Setting the move to memory

Many people feel that the most important part of learning takes place after you have been introduced to the move. Of course, the first step in learning a technique is to be exposed to it, but to be an effective athlete you must take the skill several steps farther. You must be able to hit your move or technique without thinking.

This takes practice. After learning the basic movements to your techniques, you will have to memorize them by practicing. Repetition is the key. Master the technique. Practice the skill so much that you commit the move to muscle memory. Then, think about when you would use the move. How does it fit into your system, set of techniques, or strategies? You must then decide when you are going to employ it.

Coaches can use the styles, too!

Coaches can assist wrestlers in learning by

presenting and teaching to the different styles of their athletes. If you use the demonstration/model method as your dominant style, then supplement and reinforce your demonstrations with written directions that explain, and pictures that show the moves. Make sure to use different athletes as demonstration "dummies". Provide video tapes for the athletes.

If you identify an athlete as having a particularly strong learning style, try to teach him in that modality. If you find an athlete with a weak style, don't fight with him. He's probably not trying to be difficult. He just needs some help in getting the information presented in a style he can understand. Work to teach to his strength. Use the style that effectively reaches the athlete.

Closing

So, if you want to become that champion, you will have to learn your moves and your rules. There are several different ways to learn because there are different styles of learning and thinking.

Wrestlers can usually be grouped into 3 learning styles and 2 thinking styles. It will help if you can identify your style and learn to utilize your strengths while developing complementary techniques.

There is a basic process of learning and wrestlers can benefit by following the series of: focus, watch, listen, practice the motion, master the skill, commit to memory, then enjoy.

Your coach will be your feeder, but you must take the bite. You know the old saying, "You can take a horse to water, but you can't make him drink." As a coach, I can show you the moves and tell you the rules, but I can't make you learn. That action must come from within you. And you will be much better off if you <u>decide you want to learn</u>.

So, if you are an oral person, hear my words. If you are a visual learner, see what I'm saying. If you are a kinesthetic wrestler, then take some time and try out the theories. Global thinkers should get the total picture, and if you are analytical, make an outline of the steps. Whatever you do, think about what I have said and apply it to your style and situation. If possible, use all of the styles to reinforce your learning; then forget it! Make these ideas become so much a part of your thinking that they are automatic.

Once you have prepared yourself to learn, you have made the task twice as easy. This allows you to quickly add more moves, strategies, and skills to your wrestling toolbox, thereby making you a better, closer-to-being-a-champion wrestler.

Dan Chandler, coach of the 1995 USA World Greco Team has his athletes watching, listening and feeling as he demonstrates and explains a specific situation.

Chapter 17

Drill
If
You Will

Focus: Hate to drill? You are not alone. Complaints about the drill time needed to master a skill have been floating through the practice room for years. Why do you need to drill?

Coach walks into the room. He takes you through a quick warm-up and then asks you to drill. "Drill?" you say, that questioning tone showing in your voice. You want to scrimmage. You hate drilling. You think, "I wish he would let us play; just let us roll around. Why do we have to drill? It's boring and just a waste of time. We have to do the same ole thing, time and time again. Over and over. One, two, three, four. One, two, three, four. Step, lift, turn, finish. Step, lift, turn, finish. What's the use?"

Does everybody need it?

Drilling is the key to learning physical movements. In most sports we call it practice, and it is essential. Look at baseball. How many times will players just throw the ball back and forth in an effort to learn how to throw? How many swings will be made at an invisible ball in an effort to learn how to swing? In basketball, how many practice shots will be taken at the goal; how many freethrows practiced before the athlete masters the skill? And it is the same in cross country. How many miles are run in an attempt to get everything just right?

Yet, coaches often have trouble convincing young wrestlers that drilling is the key. Most kids want to practice by having full speed scrimmages. They enjoy the play, and it makes practice fun.

"So, what's wrong with that?" you ask.

Nothing, except that research has shown that it is more productive to learn a skill first, then master it at a higher speed before we use it in competition. We don't see baseball players going into the game without knowing how to swing. We don't see gymnasts trying new tricks in the middle of competition. We don't see divers inventing dives in the middle of their contests.

What we should see in wrestling matches are athletes attempting moves that they have already mastered in the practice room--moves that are well rehearsed, ones that the athletes have confidence in performing. These are the skills and moves that occur almost automatically, without much thought or mental energy. And there is only one way to consistently do that--You Must Drill!.

Learning a move

There are certain steps to be taken in learning a wrestling move. To be successful at mastering a move, the wrestler needs to:

1) Focus on the activity. Watch and listen to its demonstration.

2) Absorb the information through the visual and auditory channels.

3) Think about the skill.

4) Repeat it.

5) Master the skill by drilling. Drilling the action or skill allows you anchor it into your nervous system.

What do we mean by "anchoring it to your nervous system"? That's just a fancy way of saying that you should practice the move so much that your body learns to responds almost automatically. You learn the series of movements so well that when you think "now" or "shoot", your body performs without having a second thought.

Take a moment and think about a simple duck-under. What do you have to do to complete that move? How many steps are there? There are probably too many to think about while you are doing the move. To overcome this, your body learns to "chunk" or group ideas. If you have really "learned" your duck, your body will "just do it" without having to think: 1) step in, 2) lower my level, 3) swing my cornering leg around and behind, 4) penetrate my hips, 5) head in tight, 6) knock him down. Once you master the skill, you will just think "duck" and

Whomp! There it is!

Muscle memory

There is an idea that many coaches label *"muscle memory"*. That is the concept that our body can memorize or learn specific movements as a group, without having to actually spend mental energy in thinking about each movement. This skill is extremely important when we try complicated or involved movements. Imagine a springboard diver or ice skater trying to think about every little position that their body needs to be in to successfully complete a dive or a movement.

Just for fun, think about what you need to do to hit a baseball. Picture your stance. Where does everything go? Now, practice your swing. What do your wrists do? Your arms? Hand? Feet? Your eyes? Which way does your head move? Your legs? Your hips?

Get the picture? You have to do too much too quickly to actually think about every movement. You don't really have an opportunity to think that fast in a competitive situation, so you must count on *chunking* or grouping the movements together in your muscle memory, then letting it happen all at once, without thinking.

Experts agree

When you talk to successful, elite-level wrestlers about drilling, they all say the same thing. James (JJ) Johnson, 220 pound Greco-Roman national champion and World Cup silver medalist, supports the idea of drilling. He says, "I drill a lot--60-70, maybe 80 times on a move in a single practice session. I use drilling as a major portion of my workout. The drilling helps me grow and I try to drill for perfection."

"When I drill, I start slowly, going through my techniques, then I work to build my speed. At least half of each workout is devoted to drilling. Sometimes I drill by myself, going through the moves without a partner. I just visualize what I want to do--which set-up I want to use--whether to throw him or bump him down. Other times I drill with a partner. Here I 'Drill To Feel'. I drill, feeling my partner's weight, his reactions, and how he would move in that situation."

Successful high school coaches agree. Ron Gray, Dowling High School, West Des Moines, Iowa, says, "We use drilling to allow the athletes to develop their fluidity. We start with slow steady drills. Through repetition their speed will pick up. When it comes down to it, there is no better way for athletes to develop their techniques. There is an old saying *perfect practice makes perfect.* I believe in this. Our wrestlers drill to make the moves instinctive, to develop that action-reaction response where the move just happens, almost instinctively."

How to drill

The idea is to start slowly, learn the move, then progress to match intensity. Many people use the whole-part-whole method. That is where you work on learning the move as a whole first, then practice the parts. You get the idea of what the move looks like and when it would be used. Then you work on its parts, correcting any little problems that you may have. Next, you practice the whole move as a complete motion, getting better and faster.

So, to use this method you would:

1) Get the total picture of when and how to use the move.
2) Practice the complete move to get the general feel.
3) Practice parts or segments of the move.
4) Tie these segments together.
5) Practice the complete move, mastering it and getting quicker.

At first, rhythm is more more important than speed. As you improve, you can begin to hit move as quickly as possible, while staying under control. Work on completing the whole move. If there are problems or if you feel some part of the move is out of whack, then work on that part. Drill your step, level change, penetration, or corner turn until it feels "right", then practice the whole move.

You can drill in several situations. 1) Drill to warm up. Start slowly, then work up a good sweat. This will get you ready to perform. Many people are now using this method to warm up, instead of doing a long stretching warm-up. 2) Drill to master the technique. Practice to be perfect. Repeat the move dozens of times. 3) Drill for conditioning. Drill hard, drill fast, and drill a lot. Work to raise that pulse into your target zone and pop out those repetitions.

Live action

Of course, live scrimmages should also be included in your training program. Moves must be practiced at match levels of intensity and speed for them to be of use in a competition. Without this level of practice, you will have trouble performing a move at the right time, with the right feeling. But care must be taken not to overtrain by sparring or scrimmaging. This intense type of practice sets the body up for injury and excessive wear and tear.

Drill new moves at a controlled pace until there is some mastery of the skill, then begin to put the move into your practice series. Balance drilling with sparring, but drill all of your moves to keep them crisp. Your body can become rusty if you ignore drilling, but you can also lose that feel for competition if you fail to include live sessions in your program.

So?

So, get a good attitude about drilling. Understand that repetition is the key to learning--it is essential that you drill if you want to learn to be a competitive wrestler. Building that muscle memory allows you to perform without thinking about every little movement.

By chunking the movements into groups, you will be able to perform each set with little or no thought. By committing many moves to your memory, you will have the answer to the different situations that may occur in your matches.

Most experts agree that their best performers are the ones who drill. The athlete who masters his moves and then commits his arsenal to automatic responses will be the one who has the best chance to react to the changing situations that occur so quickly on the wrestling mat. And that athlete will be the one who usually succeeds in having his hand raised when it is all over!

Even National Champs and World Team members drill! Randy Couture sets up to toss Matt Ghaffari's as they drill under the watchful eyes of the US Olympic Training Center's Resident Greco Coach, Anatoyli Petrosyan.

Chapter 18

"THE HENDRIX TRIDOT SYSTEM" For Penetration

Focus: Here's a set of drills that will get you moving into your foe with a good penetration step, then help you to turn that corner.

Teaching a wrestler how to finish a duck-under or high crotch can be tricky. Athletes usually understand the idea of freezing the opponent, dropping a level, and then trying to move behind. The major problem tends to be the wrestler's outside leg, the leg that goes around/behind. Instead of stepping around and behind, then dropping the hips in tight, wrestlers tend to swing the leg out wide, then try to get behind. This causes a gap to open between the wrestlers' hips, and allows the defensive man room to maneuver or counter. It feels safe to the offensive wrestler, but he now needs two more steps to finish the move.

Solution
I use a visual aid to assist the wrestlers in getting the picture of turning the corner or finishing their penetration. It is called the triangle-dot system, or *tridots* for short. This system gives the athletes a focal point for placing their feet. (After all, if it's good enough for the dance studios, it should be good enough for us.)

Marking the mats
The first step is to mark your mats with a number of triangles. Make the triangles about eighteen inches long on each side. Call this the danger zone. (Adapted from

USA Wrestling). This triangle marks the position of the defensive wrestler.

Next, place focal points to assist the wrestlers.
1) Place two yellow dots in front of a broad side of the triangle. This is the starting position for the offensive wrestler. 2) Place a red dot about a foot and a half to the side of the defensive wrestler's feet. 3) Place a green dot on the leading edge of the triangle, and one behind the triangle's back point. The completed visual aid should look like this:

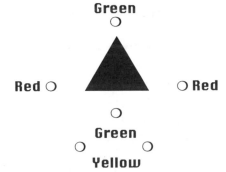

Completed Tridot Station

These triangles offer two benefits. First, they give the wrestlers a focal point for assistance in finishing their moves. Second, they mark a zone or area for each pair of wrestlers. This gives the coach some proximic control. It shows the athletes where to start each task, and it helps keep the paired athletes in separate areas. Your practice room should become more organized after placing the triangles on the mats.

Using the System

So, you have your mat marked. What now?

Have the offensive wrestler work into the danger zone; *step on the first green dot with a short penetration step.* (Some coaches call this "cheating in".) The idea is to teach your athlete to get as close as possible before he initiates an attack.

Next, have the offensive wrestler lower his level and

penetrate. For turning or cornering moves, focus on turning the outside leg toward the farthest green dot. If the lead foot lands near the red dot, the athlete and coach should recognize that the wrestler is not getting a good turn in his penetration step.

The offensive wrestler's head helps turn the corner by applying pressure to opponent's side/back. The hips are used to bang or capture the opponent's hips, so encourage the offensive wrestler to drop his levels and stay in close.

We use the tridots to drill our high crotch, duck under, arm drag, slide by, and double leg series. As the athletes are drilling, we encourage them to be aware of their foot placements. (On the high crotch series, focus on pivoting the outside knee to the green dot.)

Problems

There are several problems to look for in the wrestler's technique:

1) Stepping in too far on a cornering move. The offensive man can't turn the corner if he steps too far into the triangle. That is great penetration, but does not work well for cornering moves such as the duck, arm drag, or high crotch. If he is in "deep", he should finish his double leg, inside trip, or body lock.

2) Stepping too far outside (landing near the red dot). This causes a big gap to form between the wrestlers and allows the defensive man time and room to react.

3) Dropping the head instead of lowering the hips. This poor level change technique leaves the hips behind the body and causes bad balance.

4) Not using the head as a lever. This leaves room between wrestlers and allows the defensive man to square up, cross face, or whizzer.

5) Leaving the trail leg (lazy leg) in front of the opponent instead of completing the move. This causes the offensive man to be extended and keeps him from completing his turning movement.

Using "basic skill" vocabulary

For directed drilling (where the coach calls out the

steps), you can include the "seven basic skills" terms in your directions. An example for the duck-under would be: "Offensive man is doing a duck-under on my commands. Defensive man is a good dummy. Stance, motion, step into the triangle, make a window, drop your level, penetrate, turn the corner, lift or knock 'em down, cover the hips. Okay, good! Now remember to cut in tight, head grazes the body, hips bang hips, step to the green dot."

By walking your men through the moves a number of times, they will get the idea. As the season progresses, allow them to conduct the drills on their own. Wrestlers must learn to perform by muscle memory. There is just not enough time to think about every phase of an offensive move, so we must allow them to develop their own self-talk for each move.

Remediating or correcting

The tridot approach can be used with all levels of athletes. It is great for the beginners, but experienced wrestlers also see tremendous improvement when placed on the system. If an experienced athlete begins to float outside on his shots or starts to shoot from too far out, we will send him over to a triangle.

"Drop your level, penetrate, stay tight, and turn the corner. Ease onto the first green dot, drop your level, penetrate, then step to the back green" is a common set of directions that can help these athletes. Soon you will see them begin to make contact and turn the corners again.

Some costs involved

There is a small cost in buying the dots and supplies. Most business or department stores have the dots. They are used to code folders and envelopes, or to post prices. Training/athletic tape can be used for the triangle lines. Cover the designs with mat tape, as this keeps them anchored to the mat and gives them greater longevity.

Time is the number one expense. It takes a few of days of practice to get the athletes used to the set-up.

Like anything new, it takes a while to become familiar, but once you begin to use the system, you will notice a quick improvement. The athletes will learn to automatically go to their triangles and use them as a starting area. You will the see the wrestlers begin to focus on turning the corner and trapping the hips. After a while, you will notice them attempting that quick little turn that is needed to complete the duck or high crotch.

Closing

So, if you are trying to find a way to move in tight before shooting, or if you want a method that helps you finish turning the corner, then try these inexpensive but effective visual approaches. By encouraging your wrestlers to step in tight, penetrate, then turn that corner, you will surely add to their takedown prowess. This could be the little bit of technical support that your men need to reach a higher level of competition. Or, as we say in our practice room, "Let the tridot help you hit the spot!"

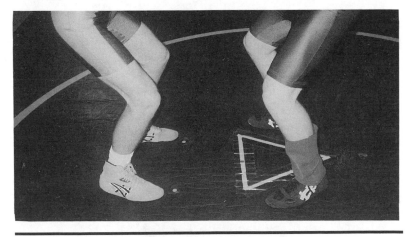

Setting up to use the system
Position your athletes. Have the defensive athlete stand over the triangle, broad side of the triangle facing the offensive man, feet placed along side the converging lines of the triangle. Offensive man positions himself in front of his opponent, on the yellow dots.

If a foot lands near red zone, the athlete has not rotated
his hips. Have him focus on turning the corner and
stepping to the back dot.

Chapter 19

Heat
Is
An Enemy

~~~~~~

Focus: Most of us have to cut weight. Even the smallest cut can upset our thinking, affect our physical well being, and play havoc with our lives. Do you do it right?

~~~~~~

Put on your sweats and get to work; there is weight to cut. You pile the bags and clothes on your body and start to work. It's hot and it's nasty. You dread going through the same ole thing, but you have to. You've got to make weight, one more time !

You work for about half an hour, then you really feel the heat. It begins to take over your thinking. Sweat drips. Dripping. Dripping down your arm, off your nose, into your eyes. Dripping off of your body. You wipe your face and shake out your sweat suit. You are miserable.

Negative thoughts run through your mind. You get angry. "Don't ask me anything. Just leave me alone." "What are you looking at?" "I don't care." Negative statements are soon flying from your lips as you fall into your new heat-inspired personality.

You want to, but...

Many athletes begin weight-cutting day by putting on their sweat suits. They work out for a short period, then begin to suffer from heat exhaustion. Yes, they work hard. Yes, they sweat like crazy. But then, their body closes down, and they can't go on. They want to, but they just can't. They sit down, undress, wipe off-- and then are worthless for the rest of the practice. Soon, they become hostile, angry, or argumentative.

At most, they were able to complete about half of the workout before having to retire. They were able to cut some water, they pulled a little weight, but at what expense? Isn't there a better way to make weight than to use excessive heat to induce rapid water loss?

The tortoise and the hare

There once was a silly hare who needed to make weight for his match. He was on weight for his weekend tourney, but had taken a big bounce. You know the kind. Saturday, after weigh-ins, he pumped down two bottles of energy drink, three oranges, and a bag of cookies. He continued to eat all day Saturday, then on Sunday he feasted on junk and even went to the all-you-can-eat pizza joint. Unfortunately, on Monday, he returned to practice 14 pounds over!

Hare's team-mate, Turtle, tried a different approach. He made weight for the weekend event, then watched his intake--no revenge eating, no buffets, no pigging out, just good balanced meals and a sensible amount of food. He hit Monday's practice about seven over.

Rabbit cut his 4 pounds-a-day at practice, but he feasted each night, so he took a bounce. Hey, he knew he could sweat it off. Ole Turtle cut his 4 pounds a day, too, but he kept his bounce under better control by following a wise diet plan.

Thursday was time to make weight again, time to check the scales and make that last effort to be on weight for the weekend's event. "Oh, my goodness," said Hare, coming into the practice room, "I'm still 8 over. Coach, I can't practice. I'll have to run. I'll never make it unless I sweat like crazy. Give me my bags. I need my sweats. Where's my jacket? Cut up the heat!"

Turtle was only about 4 over. He knew that he could cut the weight with a sensible approach. He went into the practice room and drilled for a while. He loosened up, chatted with some buddies, and basically had a good time. After about an hour, he checked his weight. Still a couple of pounds over, he decided to run. He eased on out to the road and began to jog his pace. He could see Hare sitting on the curb, head bowed, dripping with sweat.

"What's up, silly rabbit?" said Turtle.

"Dead-gummit, it's just too hot. I'm drained. I don't know if I can make it. This really stinks," said the rabbit, his eyes rolling and tongue hanging out.

As Turtle eased by on his final lap, he looked over to the hare and said, "Slow but steady makes the weight!"

"You know what you can do," weakly said Hare. He had reached the point where he would have to decide to tell coach he wasn't going to make it, or to suffer through the next 15 hours hungry, thirsty and mad.

We all know the results. Turtle jogged on around the trail and steadily made his weight while Hare tried to sprint around for another pound or two, passed out from heat exhaustion, and had to lie down under a tree to recover. He finally made his weight, but was so sucked down and miserable that he was pummeled out in the first round and didn't even make the wrestle backs.

Reverse your thinking

Are you guilty of "weighting" until the last moment, then trying to melt it off with excessive heat and exercise? If so, maybe it's time for you to try a different approach. Give the tortoise approach a try. Make your weight over a longer period of time and quit relying on rapid water loss.

Research and studies of weight reduction have proven time and time again that there is danger in rapid weight loss and dehydration. We are taught that rapid weight loss has many negative side effects and at worst can kill! Yet, go to any wrestling practice room and you will see the plastic or nylon bags, kids making sweat boxes, wrestlers rolling up in the mats, or athletes planning to hit the sauna or whirlpool after practice.

What can you do?

Try a longer, less intense practice. Many athletes get hung up on cutting those last pounds quickly. They lose sight of the fact that they have a 2 hour workout in front of them. Can any human constantly survive 2-3 hours in a plastic suit or sauna? Sure, many of you do it, but you suffer. And many athletes harm their performances by using such methods.

So, try reversing the procedure. Work your regular warm-up program, go through the first half of practice like normal, then, if you are still over, put on your sweats. That will give you a good 1 hour of work. Then you can make the last half of practice your sweat work.

You may only need to cut a pound or two, and you can surely do that in an hour. You may not even have to over-dress with plastics and layers of sweats. And it may keep you from having to suffer from those dangerous, passive, and illegal weight-loss techniques, such as the use of a rolled-up mat, sauna, or whirlpool.

Simple math

By using the old method, the wrestlers work in their sweat outfit for 25-30 minutes, then start to have heat problems. They cut very little weight in that time, so they began to panic. Nasty thoughts run through their minds. They look at the clock and start to think that they will never make it. Personalities change. They can even have rages that make them look antisocial and barbaric.

Working hard for an hour or so without the excessive heat, then putting on the sweats for a half hour, gives us 1 1/2 hours of work. It allows an athlete to continue the first half of practice in a normal routine, and allows his body to heat and cool itself naturally. This gives a wrestler time to work on techniques and skills. It also allows him to have a better practice with less physical stress involved.

Physical stress

There are several things that cause the stress felt by the weight reducing wrestlers. One is the physical stress of cutting the weight. The mere attempt to cut weight sends warning messages to the brain. Think about it. The body is not getting enough food, so it says, "Whoah. Stop this craziness. I want some calories." Your body does not want to die, so it tells you to eat. You start to get those nagging pains in your stomach and those mysterious cravings.

Dehydration also adds to the stress. The body notices that it does not have enough fluid. This sets off an alarm, and you become thirsty. Your body reacts to not having enough water.

Heat is also an enemy when it comes to cutting weight. When you get too hot, a warning light comes on. Your body begins to shut down, so it won't suffer any permanent damage. This shutdown shows itself as a nagging discomfort and a need to stop moving.

What you might have realized is that wrestlers put all three of these physical stresses together in a typical weight cutting week. You stop eating regular meals. You cut your water intake. You use heat to help reduce. As the time of truth approaches, you are hungry, dehydrated, and hot. And what kind of mood are most weight cutting wrestlers in?

Mental stress

Another type of stress is the mental stress of knowing that you have to make the weight. Many people are counting on you, so you want to do it. But there is some uncertainty. Will you be able to do it? What will they think if you don't?

This causes you to worry. You began to look into the future for answers that you can not find. "How much time do I have?" "I'm losing a pound an hour, will I make it?" "How much will I float overnight." "God, I just can't stand this!" Fear of failure begins to show its ugly face and you begin to despair.

These physical and mental stresses join together to put a double whammy on you. You are hungry, hot, dehydrated, and worried. So, what does this do to your personality? Your outlook on life?

Your choice

Your coach gives you advice, Mom and Dad tell you where they stand, and the trainer has explained to you the proper facts. It is up to you to make the right choices. These people can't ride shotgun with you for your entire athletic experience. You will have freedoms and free time when you will have to make your own decisions. If you chose to follow the wise trail, then you will need discipline and intelligence. On the other hand, if you choose to take the hard road, then you will be faced with discomfort, pain, and possible danger.

I read a quote in Anthony Robbin's book *UNLIMITED POWER* that could be applied to wrestlers who want to be champions. It said, "There are only two pains--the pain of discipline, and the pain of regret." Now that is a simple statement that holds so much truth for highly competitive athletes. It tells it like it is. You will either fight through those moments of temptation to break training, or you will regret it and feel bad about your lack of discipline.

Conclusion

Making weight is a very negative part of our sport. The methods of safe weight control have been reported and should be available to all wrestlers. Despite the abundance of these reports, there remains a mentality that says we must cut the weight as late and as fast as possible. Common practice has wrestlers making their weight, then bouncing back, only to use excessive heat in the form of plastic bags, saunas, workout room heaters, rolled-up mats, or whirlpools to sweat it off again.

These methods are not healthy and should be avoided. Other alternatives are available which include: maintaining your self discipline, setting realistic goals, and using intelligent weight control methods.

There is some comfort in knowing that you can get support from your team-mates, coaches and family, but neither coaches, research findings, nor your mother can make those hard weight-cutting decisions for you. The majority of these decisions must come from you. You must decide what and when to eat, and how much and what type of work-outs to do.

So, the consequences of these actions will rest upon your shoulders. Your level of performance, your happiness, and your safety and well-being will depend upon your choices. Let's hope that you will heed the warnings to use common sense and an educated approach in your future weight cuts.

Chapter 20

Obsession
With
Food

Focus: I only ate a salad and had a glass of juice. I swear! (Wrestler talking to coach after weighing-in four pounds over.)

How's your weight? You making it pretty good? What have you had to eat? They all seem to ask the same thing, "Are you going to make it?" Coach asks if you are close to weight. Your mom wants you to eat. Your friends are all eating ice cream and drinking sodas.

You know what you have to do. You have got to watch it, and you just hate it. Cutting weight is a such a drag! But you just can't get that food off your mind. You want to eat. You like to eat. You feel like you need to eat. Please, let me eat!

Are you really that hungry? Why are wrestlers always so obsessed with food?

Food. Food. Food!

Obsession with food is a common problem among all dieters, not just wrestlers. It is based upon a physiological reaction within your body. According to nutrition experts this is your body saying, "Hey, don't forget about me. I need some nourishment down here."

The physical disruption and discomfort are probably multiplied by the environmental and sociological events that are occurring around you.

"Say what?" you ask.

I said environmental and sociological events that occur around you may also affect your thinking. You know. Environmental things--things like television ads for food, candy, and soft drinks. You could also add billboards, signs that say "Eat at Joe's" restaurant on every corner, and other advertisements that encourage you to have additional caloric intake! These are temptations that you see or hear a hundred times a day, and they have definite affects upon your lifestyles.

Then there are also the social events, the people you hang with who are constantly eating, drinking, or talking about food. That's normal in our world. Many of our social events are centered around food and drinks.

Now add to that the fact that you are also being psychologically stressed by the desire to win and the mental pressures of making the weight. Hey, no wonder some wrestlers feel over-loaded with anxiety!

So, if you are afflicted by this dilemma, what can you do?

Obsession

According to *Introduction To Psychology* (Charles G. Morris), an *obsession* is any thought that keeps reoccurring even when a person tries to stop thinking the thought. Obsessions can cause anxiety and constant worry. It is bad enough when thoughts keep popping into our minds, but when they are worrisome, it doubles the trouble. To add to that, often the victim of obsessive thinking begins to <u>worry about worrying</u>. Talk about overloading your stress levels!

Obsessions can cause people to act unusual or to do inappropriate things. If these problems become large enough, you may have to resort to one of the choices promoted by my high school science teacher: adapt, migrate, or perish!

Dealing with obsessive thinking

Are there ways we can deal with these types of thoughts? Yes, fortunately there are some tactics that you can employ that may get you through these times of obsessive behavior. If you can recognize your obsessive thinking, you can take action that may help relieve some of the concern, worry, or pain that can be associated with that type of problem.

Adapt. You may be able to redirect your thoughts to more rewarding, or at least more pleasant areas. If you begin to feel physical anxiety because of a certain situation, you may want to go through a short relaxation script. See if the act of relaxation can remove you from focusing on the obsession. If so, you are lucky, for you have found a simple and free treatment. Unfortunately, most athletes are not able to control obsessive thinking by simply relaxing. They must use other methods.

Migrate. If it is possible, remove yourself from any environmental temptations or persons that may be causing stress. That means stay away from Fat Freddie, the fast food junkie., or don't go to Rita Overeater's party when you know there will be tons of food.

Adapt some more! Of course, migrating may not be possible or realistic. You may have to make other adjustments. It is not feasible to stop hanging with your friends, leave home, or quit school because you find it hard to cut weight there. You may have to talk to others and let them know how you feel. Tell your family and buddies how they can help you make it.

You may also have to change the way you are looking at the process or situation. Sometimes it is your focus or thinking that is adding to the stress. You select what you want to think about, so, you can control a lot of the ideas that flow through your mind. *Redirect your thinking* by looking at the ideas in a different light. Instead of focusing on how long it will be until you eat, think about a movie or the girl you are going to see tonight. Reframe your thoughts. You are not starving yourself to death. You are making the best weight for your body style.

Check your goals to make sure they are realistic. Often we find that athletes are goal driven. They like a challenge, but sometimes their goals or challenges are not realistic. Too much importance can be placed on an impossible situation. You place yourself in a no win position, yet you don't want to look like a failure.

Athletics have taught you that "if you try hard enough..."
Unfortunately this is not always true. It may not even be
true half of the time. There is no guarantee of any
outcome based upon how hard someone tries, so if your
goals are not realistic, you will be in for disappointments.

Problems

There are times when the dieting wrestler is a large
part of the problem. He has decided to try to accomplish
a weight that is not realistic, or to make a weight in an
unrealistic amount of time. The weight loss may be too
much or too sudden. Trying to reach unrealistic goals
sets an athlete up for failure, and the pursuing feeling of
depression and guilt.

When negative thoughts pop into your mind they will
probably center around fear of failure, uncertainty of
outcome, opinions of significant others, or just plain old
hunger. The best thing to do is to step back and think,
"What do I need to be doing right now?" Then make a
plan to alleviate the problem. If you feel lonely, then give
someone a call. If you want to binge eat, then settle for a
little.

Obsessive thinking tends to occur most often when
you are bored or inactive. Unfortunately, this is not an
uncommon state of mind among weight-cutting athletes.
They tend to be dehydrated and tired. Their body cries
for rest and many just want their minds to stay empty.
This leads them to do a lot of sitting around. During
these inactive moments the negative thoughts begin to
show.

Solutions

Each athlete will have to develop his own system to
handle obsessive thoughts. And because each athlete is
different, we must treat them that way and develop an
individual strategy for each athlete.

I have had some success with pairing or conditioning
an athlete to think of something else when he has his
obsessive thinking. This sounds strange, but it can work.

Once I had an athlete who complained of his stomach

growling. Todd came to me with a concern. He was attempting to make weight for a national event. Usually, in my role as a hypnotherapist, I am very reluctant to help with weight cutting. Many athletes are only interested in a quick method to cover the last days of their cut; they want someone to help them by suggesting that they are not hungry. Cutting weight is a nasty part of several sports, and the negative aspects far outweigh the idea of helping someone cut the weight by artificially altering their appetite. But Todd presented his problem in such a way as to interest me in trying to help.

In Todd's initial interview, he stated that his stomach was growling "a lot". He said that this growling was causing him to have negative thoughts and making him focus on eating. He said his diet was going okay, but he hated the noise and the resulting negative ideas. He asked if I could just do something about his growling.

I thought that was reasonable, so we decided to pair Todd's growl with another set of thoughts--instead of thinking about food when his stomach growled, he would think about his girlfriend! The key was to teach Todd that growling "meant" girlfriend.

We used a simple relaxation technique to set the stage for the pairing. Todd was instructed to recognize the growl; then he would think about Cindy. He imitated the growl, and then he spoke the word "Cindy". He imagined himself sitting with Cindy and talking. They would enjoy watching TV or other fun activities.

Todd liked the approach and used it. Several times during the week Todd began to laugh for no apparent reason. "You thinking about Cindy?" I'd ask.

"Yep," he would grin.

How?

So, how does this method work? It just replaces a thought with another thought. It would require you to:

1) Decide on a cue or trigger that would make you recognize your obsessive thinking.

2) Notice the thinking.

3) Change your thoughts to a more agreeable line of thinking.

So, basically the technique is to change your self-talk. Find something else "better" to focus your thoughts on!

Some people have success with just using a relaxation technique. They notice the stress, and then they go through a short relaxation method that includes a little speech or planned program of thought that temporarily covers the problem. The problem with this approach is that the negative thinking can return if your mind drifts back to the topic, and that is not unusual. There was a reason you were thinking about the topic in the first place. That reason is probably still hanging around in the back of your mind so it is a good possibility that your thinking will return to that spot!

Conclusion

Obsessive thinking can cause negative events to occur. You may find yourself focused on one topic for too long; so long that it begins to bother your thinking or performances. When this occurs, learn to shift your thinking to a more productive line of thought.

Not easy

So, you will have to train yourself. Work to make everything fit your approach. Remove anything that interferes. If you can't stay around candy and soft drinks, then remove them from your refrig or pantry, or just don't go looking for them. If your friends are doing something that you can't tolerate, then discuss it with them. If you are able to control your thinking, then reward yourself for adherence.

If this becomes too great a problem then take the hint. You may have designed a program that is not realistic for your situation. Examine your goals. Make sure they are realistic. A young athlete should not have his whole life controlled by negative thoughts and worry.

If you notice your obsessive thinking, then redirect your thinking, relax, and work to get off that topic.

Chapter 21

Tennis Ball Drills For Penetration and Cornering

Focus: Work on the kinesthetic approach to learning. Several simple drills will train you to stay in stance and use proper position.

Stance. It is listed as skill <u>number one</u> in our "basic skills" literature. Wrestling technique books tell you to keep a good stance. Coaches preach the topic. Video tapes show the correct ones. Yes, wrestlers are always reminded to keep a good stance, yet, many wrestlers still have problems developing and maintaining this "good stance".

So, how do you learn a good stance? What can you do to develop a stance and how can you learn to keep good body position as you perform your wrestling techniques? These are good questions that have several answers.

Athletes can use several methods to assist them in learning stance. They can watch their coach and then replicate the demonstration. They can read or watch a video. They can even ask a partner to offer them feedback. All of these methods have proven some success, but there may be a way to take a giant step closer to developing that *killer stance*.

Feel it, don't just watch or listen!

The best way to learn a stance is to get into it and feel it. By good ole hard work you learn to memorize the feeling. Then you can practice it and make yourself include it as part of your technique.

So, how is it actually learned? What can a wrestler do

to get this feel? We use a simple kinesthetic awareness procedure that allows our wrestlers to focus on the correct feel of a "good" body position. It is a simple set of drills based upon using an aid to assist our wrestlers in getting that feel.

Hey, Biffy, throw me a ball!

We use tennis balls to help our athletes feel and understand the correct positions for their stance, and the pressure points for various moves. These tennis balls are used in four series of drills: 1) elbows in, 2) motion, 3) head pressure, and 4) the chest and hip pressure drills. Each drill is practiced to assist the athlete in developing kinesthetic awareness of a specific wrestling skill.

1) Elbows are our first focus. The balls are used to encourage our young athletes to keep their elbows in near the body.

2) Motion is basic skill number 2. If you can't keep a good stance while in motion drills, you will be in trouble in your matches. We do motion drills with our tennis balls to learn movement while remaining in a tough stance.

3) Head pressure is another important skill in our sport. Most good wrestlers use their head as a lever in turning moves. Others use it to block, or as a fulcrum, in moves such as a single leg or high crotch.

4) Hip pressure and body position are also extremely important when it comes to actual combat. Our Greco chest/Greco belly drill helps the athlete become aware of pressure points needed to lift and throw.

Basic drills

The wrestlers use the tennis balls to assist in learning and memorizing body positions. The drills use aids that offer kinesthetic feedback. This gives the athletes a feel for what should be going on. It reminds them which part of their body needs to stay tight or where they need to be pushing.

By practicing over and over with the devices, the athletes build a stance or penetration technique that stays with them. They 'learn' the technique by feel. Some of the drills will include exaggerated positions and unrealistic stops in your flow. That is okay. The exaggeration will emphasis what you need to do, and the stops will cause you to focus on the concept you are working on.

Drill 1: Stance-elbows in

USA Wrestling's 1994 wrestling skills tapes recommend "stance-elbows in". Most coaches tell their athletes to comply with this command. Time and time again the athletes are asked or told to keep their elbows near the body. "Don't over extend." "Don't reach." These are common commands issued by coaches. The athletes passively listen and may tuck their elbow for a second, but after a while, the elbows start to float out away from the body, opening the wrestler up for a duck-under, high crotch, or drag series.

To help alleviate this problem place a tennis balls between the wrestler's elbows and his side. He then must use pressure to keep the balls from dropping. This pressure comes from an active attempt to press the elbows in towards his side. The constant awareness of the balls between the elbows and side trains the athlete to keep a tight position. Many wrestlers even learn to pummel from this position.

Using the tennis ball drill for elbow control

To check your chest, back, and head alignment, try standing in front of the mirror and looking at your stance. Keep the balls between your elbows and side.

Your: A) head should face forward, B) chest even with knees, C) back slightly bent, D) feet--shoulder width apart.

Your hands are still able to "swim" and your arms can rotate, so give them a twirl. It should look like your elbows are tied to your torso.

Drill 2: A Moving experience

Next, begin your second basic skill--motion. You may want to start while standing in front of the mirror. You don't have to, but this offers visual clues. This drill begins by moving from side to side, remembering to keep your tennis balls in place. Practice dropping your level while you focus on your elbows. Pretty soon you will start to lose the feeling of the balls. They are there, and your elbows are tight, but you don't sense the balls. You are now ready to move to a more complicated motion drill.

To reach the next skill level, add a more complex series of motion. Learn to keep your balls in place as you drop your level and penetrate with a drop-step.

The "don't drop" step drill

We lengthen the drop-step drill to get used to moving. The athlete keeps the balls in place as he goes through a long series of drop-steps. The directions are simple: Drop-step across the mat while keeping your tennis balls in position. The balls restrict the reaching movements and limit a wrestler's balance but places tremendous focus on elbow position. This drill also keeps the athlete from attempting that infamous *airplane double* where he dives in with both arms extended from his sides like airplane wings.

We have also developed a *head swim drill*. This is just an advanced drop-step drill. We keep the tennis balls under our elbows, while we drop step with into a partner who is positioned in front of us. He slowly walks backwards as we lower our level and drop step into his triangle. Our head moves to the appropriate position as we penetrate. It takes a different position on each shot. The athlete might start with a *double leg*--his head outside, pressing in on the hip, hands around both legs. He then drop-steps into a *single leg*--head inside, hands butterflied around a leg. Next, he moves to a *high crotch*--head on the outside, pressure in, hand in crotch, other hand forming a window with the opponent's arm.

The object is to keep moving across the mat, drop stepping into your opponent, switching from move to move, without dropping the balls. We call it head swim drill because your head is constantly moving from hip to inside, then back, as you switch from move to move.

Drill 3: The magic, moving ball

Next, we move to a more advanced head swim drill, where the wrestlers use a single ball. As the wrestler shoots in on his drop steps, he puts the ball onto the proper pressure point. He keeps shooting different moves and keeps replacing the ball, moving it from position to position.

The magic ball focuses on head pressure. Head pressure is a skill that coaches "often preach but seldom teach!" They tell their athletes to "use your head", but do not push the point farther by actually making the athlete press in with his head. By using a tennis ball as a physical reminder, we are able to focus on head pressure and develop the skill.

How? The wrestler has a ball in his hand. He shoots into his move and pauses a moment to place the ball at it proper point of pressure. He then completes his move while focusing on the head pressure point.

For a double leg, place the ball on the outside hip. The ball is positioned between your head (ear) and your partner's hip or thigh. Press in to keep the ball in place. Think about the pressure point you use on a double.

You also use the ball to focus on your turning motion. On a high crotch place the ball outside on your partner's hip. Make sure to get it in a position that replicates where your head presses when you shoot your high crotch. As you rotate your leg around and behind, note the pressure that needs to be applied to your opponent's body. If your head pops out too soon, your foe can bring his near side hip around and square off, or center on you and stop you from slipping in behind. This will change your angle of attack and require you to go into a lifting or battling position.

If the ball falls out before you start your turn, you may have a bad angle of attack. Your head could be driving out away from your opponent's body at a 45 degree angle that actually takes you away from your goal of penetrating and turning the corner.

For your single leg place the ball between your ear and your partner's inside thigh. Keep the ball in place, swim your butterfly grips and change hand positions.

Your stance, motion, level, penetration skills are all drilled as your head moves from side to side, move to move.

Drill 4: Dancing at the ball

The athletes also use the tennis balls to assist them in their Greco pummelling. This is a fun series of drills that we call "dancing".

The first we call a *high chest* drill. Have the athletes stand chest to chest. Place a single tennis ball on the wrestlers' sternum. They then begin to pummel in for a bear hug. The object is to keep the ball between their chests, and they do this swimming action. This reminds the wrestlers to keep contact.

Belly button fighting is the same as high chest, except that the ball has been lowered to the belly button area. Athletes stand with their belly buttons touching. Place a ball between their bellies. Let them begin to pummel. They then try to get into lifting position without losing the ball.

Playing hard ball

Use old tennis balls. New ones are too hard. If you want, slice a hole into each ball. This makes it a little softer, as it lets air escape if the ball is compressed. For the less manly-men, you might try bean bags, but finding enough bean bags is probably harder than getting your tennis coach or local tennis pro to donate a box of old balls to your team. (We have about 100 balls to use with our athletes.)

Cautions

As you may have already guessed, the air can become filled with missiles. It always seems that there is a joker or two in every group. A knuklehead will want to toss the balls at someone, and the coach will have to deal with that. Beware! Even coaches can become the target of a sneak attack!

You also need to be cautious as to twisting an ankle on a wayward ball. When you have 100 or so balls out, as we do when we drill, you must be careful. A misplaced ball can grab a wrestler by the foot and cause a nasty ankle turn. We always put the balls back in the box as soon as we are finished. This takes care of both of these problems.

Closing

Almost every athlete can benefit from these drills. They are easy to follow and help the athlete to form the muscle memory needed to carry out the skill without having to waste mental energy thinking about what to do. By offering kinesthetic awareness and over-exaggerating certain concepts, you train the athletes' bodies to hold the proper position and produce the correct pressure.

The biggest problem is in getting the athletes accustomed to managing their tennis balls. Once the wrestlers see how much these drills assist them in their skills, it becomes easier. They will cut out the horse play. You may even see your athletes begin to use the balls on their own as they drill their shots before or after practice.

Tennis Ball Drills

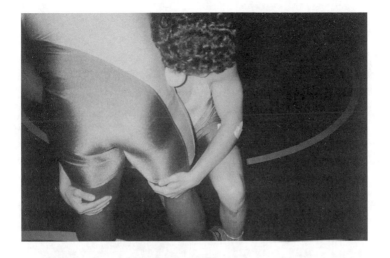

For a double leg or high crotch, the pressure is on the outside. Head presses in on the ball.

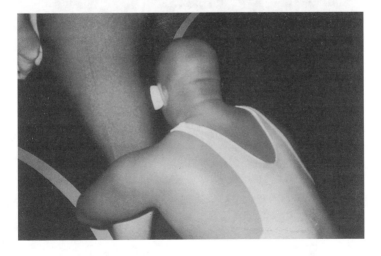

For a single leg, the pressure point is on the inside. Head presses out on the ball. Hands pull in giving resistance to the head pressure.

Other Ideas

Off the mat athletes can gain additional knowledge by reading, studying, or even by talking to experts. The library often holds a wealth of information.

Section IV

Other Ideas

Articles

Centuries of combat have produced a tremendous amount of battle strategies. What can we learn from the ancient warriors who wrestled with death in thousands of military engagements? The wisdom of these warriors may enhance your strategies and help in your performances.

You can find wrestling information in some of the strangest places. Why not recruit the librarian to help? We did, and found that wrestling with the librarian is fun!

Goal setting is a favorite topic of coaches and psychologists. The ideas behind goals and goal setting are offered.

In the end was the beginning, and it was good. The end of your season is just the beginning of next year. Have you done what it takes to crank it up for the upcoming off-season and then the next year?

So how would a team use this sport psychology and mental skills information? We developed a way to include the skills at my schools.

Now, take a moment to look back at the major ideas. This will prepare you for your next task. You are the sport psychology consultant. What will you do?.

Chapter 22

Wisdom
of the
Ancient Warriors

Focus: You have two eyes and two ears, but only one mouth. Look and listen at least twice as much as you talk and you will be much better off.

It is late in the second period of the championship match, and you are behind. On your feet, you are attacking, but you can't score. Your opponent just hasn't taken any chances and he has kept a great stance. The flurry takes you out of bounds, so there is a short break in the action as you walk back to the center of the mat. You look over to your coach for help, but something weird happens. He transforms into what looks like a magnificent Chinese warrior of ancient times. He is wearing beautiful silk robes, a helmet, and a sword hanging from a fancy sash, and he looks just like your idea of a Oriental general!

You are startled and feel a tingling sensation throughout your whole body. You must be dreaming, but you need some ideas fast, so you ask, "What do I do now?" a little panic showing in your voice.

The ancient warrior speaks

"It is very simple, my young warrior. You must first lure the tiger out of his mountains," the general offers, his voice crystal clear.

Tiger, mountains, old Chinese guy? Boy are you in trouble! You wonder what it all means, but it suddenly hits you. Your opponent is sitting in a great stance and you are attacking him head-on, from the front. But, he is too strong there. To succeed, you must make him move out of his stance--get him out of his comfortable setting, make an angle. The general is right; you must make the tiger come to you

You hear the voice again. *"It is said that it is often possible for a wise man to create something out of nothing."*

You understand. You really don't have to finish a technique. If you can just make your foe move, that will open his stance, and then you will have your chance. But how? You don't want to attack him head-on again. A new thought enters your mind. *"Ahh, my young battler, feint to the east, while attacking the west. Pretend to take one path, while sneaking down another."* Yes, that's it. Fake him. By faking a move you can get him to open up, extend a little, or make a bad *step.*

"A cunning leader will beat the grass to startle the snake."

"That a boy, general!" you think. "I'll use the fake to see which way he will go. That will let me see his reaction." With that in mind, you feint towards his leg, and he drops back into a short sprawl. Now you've got it. You see his reaction and know what to do. You want to arm drag him and get behind.

"The commander who knows how to attack makes his enemy not know where to defend. If you want to do something, it is best to make your opponent do it for you."

Great idea. You will fake again towards his leg. Since you know that he will sprawl, you will shuck his arm, and finish your drag. How brilliant--and it works! You get your takedown and turn him for back points to take the lead.

Gaining confidence

But it is not over yet. It is the third period and he chooses bottom. You are up by four points. What do you do? You look to the sidelines, not knowing what you'll see or hear.

"Sometimes, warrior, we can snag the enemy by

letting him off the hook."

Catch him by setting him free? What does he mean? It hits you! You are a takedown champion: no one can take you down, especially if you just get into your stance. Just let him go and work your takedown.

"A wise army will relax while the enemy exhausts himself. Those skilled in war avoid the enemy when his spirit is keen and attack when he is sluggish."

"Right? Right!", you think. You take a good defensive stance. The enemy is going crazy, moving side to side, jumping up, dropping his levels, but you remain cool. The enemy begins to tire. He has a panicked look.

"It is said that a familiar sight provokes no attention. Misleading the enemy by false appearance, this is what strategy is all about."

Once again you hear and understand. You get back into your normal stance. You look ready, but show nothing unusual. The enemy thinks you are going to stall out. He charges, trying to lock up a throw.

"The great general Sun Tzu suggested that you should exhibit coyness until the enemy loses his alertness and gives you an opening, then move as swiftly as a hare, and the enemy will be unable to resist you. Attack the enemy where he is not prepared and you are least expected. Often, the best defense is an offense."

Yes, the enemy is too high and has left his good stance. You drop your level, rotate, and finish a high crotch. It is almost over.

"Have caution, my soldier, for of all the 36 stratagems, the ultimate is the last one--Run away. Or as Sun Tzu advised, to subdue the enemy without fighting is the supreme excellence."

Win by avoiding the fight? Man, where has this guy been all of your life? He sure knows how to battle? But, should you cut him loose?

"Know your enemy and know yourself--and you can win a hundred battles without defeat."

You know that the enemy has a good granby roll series--he hit you with it in the first period and took the lead--so, you decide to cut him loose again. Great strategy; this will allow you to win without fighting! You circle as the clock ticks its last 15 seconds.

You win! You are the champion. Boy, it is great. You look over to the general and reach out to shake his hand. He gives you a quick bow and then fades away, leaving one last thought--*"Many grains of sand piled up a pagoda make."* It is as clear as a bell. You have just put together hundreds of little thoughts and actions to build a championship match. Again the general has made his point.

"And wild times make heroes," you think as your coach's face comes back into focus.

The aftermath

"Wow," says your coach. "You were fabulous. You looked so focused; so intense. Man, you were zoning. What were you thinking?"

"Ahh, it was nothing," you say. "Nothing that a wise old coach and I couldn't handle!"

Suddenly you get that feeling, that tingling you felt earlier in the match. You turn and look. There he is, again, and he offers one last jewel. *"You have listened well, my young warrior. Now your camp will enjoy victory. Remember: When two grasshoppers are tied to one string, neither can escape."*

You think about it for a moment. "Coach, we're sorta like two grasshoppers tied to a string," you say as you turn to leave. "Both of us must suffer the same fate. We work together for the same goals so we can enjoy our victories together, or together we suffer through our defeats."

"What?" says Coach, turning to face you. "That last cross face he popped on you must have cracked your head."

"Ahh, forget it," you say, smiling. "It was just something I heard." Coach grins and gives you a hug. You both smile as you walk off of the mat.

Wisdom of the ages

Warfare has been going on for centuries, and warrior wisdom has been passed down through the years. Many great books, articles, and tales survive that offer information to today's modern warriors.

Is it too much to consider a wrestler a modern day warrior? If one thinks about it, wrestling is like war, only on a one to one basis. So, maybe these words of wisdom could be useful in the wrestling areas.

What if we could interview some of the greatest generals and warlords of the past? What would they say that could help us understand some of the strategies and ideas of wrestling? What would it be like to take a look at the wisdom that came from the minds of those ancient people?

In the preceding story you were introduced to 21 bits of wisdom that can be found in the writings of ancient Chinese warriors and thinkers. Let's look back on some of that advice and see how it lends itself to wrestling.

Take a moment to think about these ideas. What does each saying mean to you? How can they help you and your strategies? After you have interpreted them by your standards, compare your ideas to mine. The story of the championship match may give you some hints.

The wisdom of the tale

1. Lure the tiger out of his mountains.
2. Create something out of nothing.
3. Feint to the east, while attacking the west.
4. Pretend to take one path, while sneaking down another.
5. Beat the grass to startle the snake.
6. The commander who knows how to attack makes his enemy not know where to defend.
7. If you want to do something, it is best to make your opponent do it for you.
8. Snag the enemy by letting him off the hook.
9. Relax while the enemy exhausts himself.
10. Those skilled in war avoid the enemy when its spirit is keen and attack when it is sluggish.

11. A familiar sight provokes no attention.
12. Misleading the enemy by false appearance, this is what strategy is all about.
13. Exhibit coyness until the enemy loses his alertness and gives you an opening, then move as swiftly as a hare, and the enemy will be unable to resist you.
14. Attack the enemy where he is not prepared and you are least expected.
15. The best defense is an offense.
16. Of all the 36 stratagems, the ultimate is the last one--Run away.
17. To subdue the enemy without fighting is the supreme excellence.
18. Know your enemy and know yourself--and you can win a hundred battles without defeat.
19. Many grains of sand piled up a pagoda make.
20. Wild times make heroes.
21. When two grasshoppers are tied to one string, neither can escape.

Interpreted for the modern wrestling warrior

Of course there are no correct answers, only ideas and concepts that will fit your way of thinking. It is fun to look at these axioms and see if we can make them fit our world. You may want to use these to make up some of your own, then quote them at practice to make a point, sound philosophical, or just to joke.

1. Do not fight an enemy's strength. Make him fight your match.
2. Many wrestling points are scored on "no name" moves. Many moves are initiated by simple fakes, or feints (non-moves or nothings!).
3. Get your enemy to move in the wrong direction by making him react to your moves.
4 Same as above.
5. Cause a reaction. Don't wait on the snake to bite you. Make him move, then you can see what he is doing.

6. Be unpredictable and cunning. Cover your intentions. Use surprise.

7. Use setups that make your enemies move the way you want them to.

8. Often we can't turn the man from top. It may be easier to beat him by setting him free, only to take him down again.

9. A good stance with controlled motion will conserve energy as opposed to a wrestler who is tense and constantly jumping around.

10. Don't rush. If your enemy is engaged in rapid movements or in unorthodox techniques, get into a good defensive stance and allow him to settle down. When he slows back to your pace, complete a set-up, and attack.

11. Offer the same appearance as to not alarm. Don't look at his leg or drop lower when you want to attack legs. Give him the same stance and make him think you are always doing the same thing. Thus he is not alerted or forewarned to your plans.

12. Hide your intentions. Make false moves. Fool your enemy.

13. Keep your stance until you have an opening, then take it without delay.

14. If he is not expecting, he will not be ready. Look for flaws in his stance or in the way he moves. Too far forward, snap him. Standing too tall or straight up, then leg attack. Pushing? Then toss him. Take advantage of his weak areas if possible.

15. Your enemy will have problems organizing an offense if he is constantly defending against your attacks. He must fight your war.

16. Yes, there are times when we need to circle, shoot half-shots, and hold on to win. This is an accepted part of our sport, if it occurs late in the match and a wrestler has a lead. Let's hope that it does not become a bigger part of our sport, as we are constantly reminded that

stalling not only takes away from the beauty of our game, but it also makes our sport boring and helps to drive away the fans.

17. Same as above. Could also mean that technique is much better than muscle. Slick technicians appear to win without straining or fighting. They slide through their moves while musclers strain and fight to get every point.

18. If you know what your enemy can do and what you are capable of doing, you can make wise choices that will allow you to compete at your best.

19. Many small things can add up to big things. Many little steps make a long trip.

20. Heroes are not made during calm weather; they overcome great challenges.

21. People working together will share in the consequences.

These are just a few bits of ancient wisdom that may allow you to see things from a different view. You may want to incorporate them into your mind set. If you do, then good luck and have fun.

Remember: **Without the lips, the teeth would be cold!**

Credits--Sun Tzu's, The Art of War, by General Tao Hanzhang, as translated by Yaun Shibing. Lure The Tiger Out Of The Mountains, (*The 36 Stratagems of Ancient China*) by Gao Yuan.

Chapter 23

Wrestling with the Librarian

Focus: Most of us learn through different channels, yet we depend upon someone to show and tell us how to wrestle. Why not add to your knowledge by reading about our great sport?

A school's library may seem to be an unusual place to find a group of wrestlers, but an cooperative venture between a school's library media specialist and the wrestling coach has made one library a positive and comfortable place for young wrestlers to be visiting. And it has appeared to have paid off. Wrestlers there are able to locate, check out, and read material that fits their athletic and recreational reading interests.

These interests have been used to promote reading among a group that historically has been labeled "reluctant readers". By involving the librarian with the wrestling team, and the wrestling team with the media center, an unlikely partnership has cut through the normal stereotypes to produce a program that proves athletics and academics can work together to enhance the education of student-athletes.

Not only does the following story tell of a school's successful implementation of a wrestling-related reading program; it offers interested coaches, librarians, and wrestlers an outline of how they can work together to help each other. Read on and see how Coach Hendrix and his Cartersville Middle School wrestlers enticed their school librarian to join the wrestling team!

First year blues

When the CMS wrestling team began practice for the 1993-94 season, about 30 students turned out. It was the first year that the school had offered a team, so most of the students had no idea about the sport. Two-thirds of the athletes had never even seen a wrestling match. What could I do to get these athletes ready for their first season of competition?

For these youngsters to be successful, I needed to expose them to as much wrestling as possible. Wrestling practice would offer an hour and a half each day, but maybe there was a way to expose them to more information. Maybe I could supply them with reading material that would supplement their physical practices.

Librarian recruited

Knowing that my library media specialist, Mrs. Pat Turner, was always on the lookout for new ideas, I asked her if it would be possible to place a collection of wrestling magazines in the leisure reading area. I told her that it would motivate my athletes to go to the library. She liked the idea, so magazines such as Wrestling USA, Amateur Wrestling News, Scholastic Coach, and USA Wrestling were placed in a prominent area, to catch the wrestlers' attention. We also included high school wrestling programs, World Cup programs, and any state newsletters that I had. If it was wrestling related, we wanted it on the shelf.

Why the library?

The library is the perfect place. That's what a library is for-- to serve as a haven for readers and information seekers. They also have an attractive area to use. And, let's face it; if there's one thing a coach hates to do, it's organizing a system to keep up with who has what, and when it should be returned. But, the library staff does an excellent job with that. They have the means and skills to handle displaying, circulating, and tracking inventory. And, remember, they are there to help. After all, library media specialists are trained to be experts at helping!

Look. There's some wrestling books!

The wrestlers responded. They went in, saw the display, and immediately started reading the magazines. Mrs. Turner noticed that the kids began to ask, "Do you have anything else on wrestling?" She didn't, so she mentioned the requests and her lack of wrestling material to me. I had an answer for the problem--I brought in several wrestling technique books. Mrs. Turner computer coded them for inventory purposes, then placed them in the non-fiction stacks.

We now had wrestling periodicals and wrestling non-fiction books inventoried and placed in the media center. The athletes took notice; they started to check out and read the non-fiction books. We had accomplished my original goals--the wrestlers now had written information that could supplement their wrestling practices, and they were using it.

The librarian shoots a move

After seeing the results with the periodicals and non-fiction materials, Mrs. Turner realized that a natural step would be to direct the students to wrestling fiction stories. She had researched the idea of motivating reluctant readers, and now saw how this new wrestling reading program addressed several of the problems mentioned in her research. (One of the problems is that middle school males tend to be reluctant readers. They start to move away from reading and engage in other activities, such as sports.) She investigated the possibility of using wrestling books to reach a group that has been to be reluctant to read or checkout material.

Pat hoped that by focusing on a student's interest, then adding a coach's recommendations, we could promote an increase in the athletes' recreational reading. Research emphasised the importance that sports plays in this age group, and supported our idea that, with a little encouragement by educators, student-athletes may be drawn to reading by beginning with sports related information.

Pat had a resource (Sherman & Ammon, 1993) that reviewed, by subject, high interest books for reluctant teen readers. The book listed 8 fiction books that focused on wrestling topics. Pat had 4 of the books:
1) <u>Takedown</u>, by Matt Christopher; 2) <u>Rusty Fertlanger, Lady's Man</u>, by Christi Killien; 3) <u>There's a Girl in My Hammerlock</u>, by Jerri Spenelli; and 4) <u>Athletic Shorts</u>, by Chris Crutcher. Since she already had some wrestling material, the next step was to find a way to get the wrestlers to the fiction stacks to see it.

Match strategy

We designed a program that encourages the wrestlers to read. We set basic goals, using the wrestling books: 1) To assist the athletes in obtaining wrestling information, 2) To reach wrestlers who prefer reading as a learning style, 3) To introduce the athletes to pleasure reading, 4) To encourage usage of the library-media center, and 5) To nurture lifelong literacy.

But how could these goals be accomplished?

We organized an approach.

1.   The periodicals would be used as "bait". The short articles, color pictures, and varied topics fit the reading styles of the wrestlers and would catch their attention. From the periodicals (magazine) rack, we would direct the wrestlers to the non-fiction books.

2.   The non-fiction books drew the athletes to the stacks. These non-fiction books were longer and more in depth than the periodicals, but most used photographs and diagrams to show technique. They were a definite bridge between the magazines and the fiction material. This was the area that had to be utilized to direct the readers to the fiction holdings area. If the athletes would scan this material, there was hope that they could be encouraged to try the fiction works.

3.   We placed flyers among the periodicals and nonfiction material. The flyers mentioned the wrestling fiction books that we had in our media center. By focusing the athletes' attention on these books, we hoped that we could pull the wrestlers into the fiction stacks

and encourage them to browse this area, see something they liked, then check it out to read.

4.   Pat and I would encourage the wrestlers by actively taking part in the program. We agreed to perform specific tasks that would help generate interest in our idea.

Our tasks

My job was to motivate the students and to serve as a role model. I supplied the wrestling periodicals and non-fiction material, and encouraged the students to visit the library. I announced to the team that wrestling magazines had been placed in the media center, and I would periodically mention the library at practice. Sometimes I gave a short booktalk on one of the selections, and each month I placed new magazines on the shelf. This took very little time or extra effort.

Mrs. Turner organized the material and was the resource expert. She designed a comfortable reading area by the magazine display to help promote the idea. She also placed signs in this area that directed the athletes to the wrestling non-fiction section. There, she had the wrestling books grouped and marked.

Above the non-fiction grouping, she placed a sign that read:

Are you interested in wrestling?
Then, try one of these books.

The sign listed our fiction holdings that were centered around wrestling themes, and it gave a brief summary of each book on the list. To complement the sign, Mrs. Turner displayed one of the books right by the sign. This made it easy for the athletes to inspect the books.

When classes came to the library, Pat asked if any of the students were on the wrestling team. If wrestlers were present, they were directed to the books. To our joy, the books were usually checked out.

Final score

The project was successful. It increased traffic to the library media center, and increased the number of checkouts of wrestling non-fiction, and wrestling fiction books. What's more important, athletes who had shown no previous interest in reading began to check out material!

Another reward was the reaction seen on the athletes' faces. Mrs. Turner reports that many of the boys commented that they didn't like to read. She began to approach the problem by saying, "You just haven't found the right book, yet. Let me show you these." Mrs. Turner was able to give the athletes books that they really wanted to read. The students enjoyed being recognized as wrestlers. This new identity appeared to help build their self-esteem. They also noticed that the librarian had taken a special effort to find something "just for them". Pat could tell by the smiles on their faces that they were now leaving with the "right book".

Future

There are plans for the future. I have committed to locating more wrestling material and would like to continue the partnership. We want to develop a system that all library media specialists and coaches can use to encourage more and better interaction between the two professions.

Mrs. Turner is now using the system with other coaches in our school. We are getting more of the athletes involved, and the program appears to be working with these other teams. She has also committed to purchasing more sport-related material for our library.

For the coach

If you have periodicals or non-fiction material that would interest your athletes, why don't you suggest this approach to your media specialist? You might want to show her this article. You can work together to make your library media center an inviting place for your athletes, while helping them learn their sport. It may help them develop a lifelong reading habit. It could also be an opportunity to expand your resources, and maybe even get coaches some positive recognition within the academic world. (And we all know that those are two things that we really need!)

For wrestlers

Check your library/media center out. See what they have that can help you. Ask the librarian for assistance. They want to put material on the shelves that you want to read. Just let them know you will use it and they will be glad to work with you. But remember to keep your end of the bargain. If it is purchased, go and use it!

Talk to your coach. See if he can get the library to implement this project. Talk about what you would like to have. Donate magazines to the library. Have the librarian set up an area for reading. As I said before, if there is interest, the librarian will usually work with you!

Responses

The success of this reading program has been noted by many people. First and foremost are the athletes. Our wrestlers enjoy browsing through the magazines and other reading material. We feel that this encourages them to read and also makes them feel at home in the media center.

We have been surprised by the acceptance of this program by outside sources. The response has been great, and reports have ranged from local, to state, to national! It didn't sound like a really Earth-shattering hypothesis-- "Get kids books about topics they like and they will probably read more of them." But people liked the approach, the uniqueness of using sports books, and actually motivating readers through their sports teams! Since then we have accumulated some interesting kudos and recognition.

Some of the responses:
1. *Scholastic Coach,* a respected national

periodical for coaches and athletic directors, ran a four page article on the project.

2.   The *Atlanta Journal / Constitution* reported our project in their "Main Street, Georgia" section.

3.   Ohio State University's wrestling coach, Russ Hellickson, sent the media center an autographed copy of his wrestling techniques book. He included a special page of words of encouragement for Cartersville's youth. I informed Hellickson about the project, and he was happy to help.

4.   Georgia Middle School Association asked Ms. Turner to report the project in their statewide *Georgia Middle School Newsletter*.

5.   Dr. Craig Horswell, a scientist with Gatorade Laboratory, read the article in *Scholastic Coach* and was so impressed that he sent an autographed copy of his recent book on nutrition for us to include in our sports reading area. Dr. Horswell knew no one on our staff. He just liked the idea.

6.   *School Library Journal* ran an article in its December, 1994 issue reporting on the project from a librarian's point of view. This magazine is a widely circulated professional library journal.

7.   I was on a flight to the Olympic Training Center in Colorado Springs when a young man approached me. The man asked if I had written an article about encouraging athletes to read. When I said that I had, the young man identified himself as a Michigan wrestling coach who read the article and tried it in his own school. He stated that the principal, media specialist, and himself were thrilled by the interest generated by their use of our program's ideas.

We are happy with the results and hope other coaches, athletes, and librarians can join together to form reading *"teams"* in their schools. By pulling together the periodicals, non-fiction material, and fiction sides of the media center, then introducing them to the athletes, we have developed and implemented a program that proves that even the most unlikely of partnerships can sometimes be the most rewarding. As you can see, it is a project that is easy to implement and has some very rewarding results. As a matter of fact, we now have four R's:

ouR wRestlers aRe Readers!

Resources
Sherman, Gale W. & Ammon Bette D. (1993). <u>Rip-roaring reads for reluctant teen readers</u>., California: Libraries Unlimited.

We supplied our wrestlers with additional wrestling information while encouraging outside reading. We began by offering the athletes an attractive wrestling display to catch their attention.

Chapter 24

Goals and Goal Setting

Focus: What is goal setting and how does it fit into our sport? How does one set goals? Are there guidelines?

You have heard the story on goal setting. There are certain things you must do, and certain formulas you must use to be successful. It is usually proposed that if you will only follow those guidelines you will become king of the hill, a man above men, champion of the world. But does this happen? Obviously not. Everyone who reads these articles does not become world champions or automatic success stories.

Why? First, it is not possible. Everyone can't be the top man. Second, these articles often sound complicated and are too much for most people to handle. They are filled with big words and ideas. They cover the material, but they are too academic for most of us to understand.

What we really need is simple information that teaches wrestlers how to organize a system of goal setting that assists them with their competition. We need to answer the basic questions so wrestlers can use the information to improve their goals setting skills, set new and improved goals, and work toward achieving the level of performance that each wrestler sets for himself.

So, lets take a look at these basic questions and try to find some answers. What is goal setting? Why do we really need it? How do we set goals? How can wrestlers use goal setting to help them get better and enjoy the sport?

Goal setting defined

Starting a trip without knowing the destination would probably cause anxiety and tension. Where are we going? What are we going to do? How will we get there? People feel better if they know where they are going.

Goal setting goes along with this concept. The idea is that a person can achieve more if he knows where he is going. The basic idea is that a wrestler selects a destination- a place where he wants to go, then he works to reach that place. This sounds simple--pick what you want to do, and then do it! So in simple terms--*goal setting is deciding what you want to do.*

Goal setting experts have identified several basic steps in the goal setting process. They suggest that athletes follow a simple set of guidelines that will help them become better goal setters. The guidelines state: *for a goal to be effective it must be: specific, realistic, concrete, challenging, and self-referenced.*

Goal requirements

From these basic steps we develop a set of requirements which help set goals that will be beneficial for wrestlers. And these will be goals that you can achieve. Let's look at these requirements one at a time to get a feel for each.

1) *Specific.* Set a goal that has a definite result. I want to *"get better"* on my feet is not specific. What does better mean? At what? A wrestler needs to state his goal in a more specific manner. "I will try at least 6 takedown shots per minute on my feet" is a specific goal that allows you to have a definite idea of what you want. "I will take a 2 mile run 3 times a week."

2) *Realistic.* Make your goals realistic, which means: *set a goal you can reach.* Don't be overly optimistic about what you can do. "I will work out every day for 2 hours" would be a good goal for an athlete who is on summer vacation and doesn't have anything else going on. Unfortunately, most people would have problems meeting this goal. They would be discouraged

by the failure and might just stop working out at all. "I will workout 3 days a week for a minimum of 1 hour each day on my takedowns" sounds more realistic. You should be able to do something three time a week that is takedown related, even if you can't find a mat. By setting an achievable goal, you allow yourself a chance to actually meet the goal and feel good about it.

3) *Challenging.* We said the goal must be realistic to make sure it is within your reach, but we must also take care to make sure it is challenging. Your goal should offer you an interesting trip. That means it should contain work-outs and tests of achievement that will keep you fired up and happy. If your goal is not challenging, if it is too easy, you will become bored and quit.

4) *Concrete.* Make your goal something that can be measured. If we can measure the goal, we can see if it has actually been met. If it hasn't been met, we can at least see how close we got. "I want to score 2 takedowns in each period that we start on our feet" is a concrete goal. We know what a takedown is--it is a concrete concept, so we can tell if we get 2 takedowns.

5) *Self-referenced.* This big idea actually has a little meaning. It means you make the goals fit you, and your ability level. Focus your goals based upon what you can do.

Two time frames

When you hear people talk about goals they often mention the idea of *long term* and *short term* goals. This is the concept that you should set goals in order, sort of like a staircase. You reach a certain set of goals before you reach others. Think of them as small steps you reach before you are able to get to the top.

Long term goals are the destinations--the final point that you wish to reach. They are like the platform at the top of the stairs. Short term goals are the little steps that make up the trip toward your destination. An example would be: Long term goal-- "I bench 120 now. I want to bench 145 by the time season gets here." A short term goal based upon this long term goal would be: "I need to increase my bench by 6 pounds a month." You should reach your long term goal after 4 months of hard work if you are reaching your short term points. (120 plus 6 this month = 126. 126 pounds plus 6 more next month = 132 and so on.)

Good goal setting

So, good goal setters would follow this outline. They would set a final destination. Then they would have a series of small steps, a direction in which they will be going. We can think of this direction as baby steps. The athlete would make sure to abide by the rules, and set goals that were specific, realistic, challenging, concrete, and self-referenced.

We also have to set our goals with an understanding of two terms: *performance goals* and *result-based goals*. Performance goals are goals set with specific performance standards in mind. Taking at least 4 shots per minute would be a performance-based goal. Planning to use a specific setup before a takedown attempt is a performance-based goal. Taking hand control on the whistle while in the bottom position is a performance goal.

Result goals are the goals and ideas that are based on what the final score will be. Winning is a result-based goal. Finishing the season with a 12-0 record would be a result-based goal. Beating an opponent is a result goal. We all use result-based goals and they can motivate us, but it is hard to control the results of a contest. Our opponent, the ref, luck, and several other factors have something to do with the outcome, so we actually have very little control over it.

With performance goals we can at least set goals for things we can control. I know I can hit 35 back arches in practice. I know I can climb the rope 5 times after practice. I know I can practice shooting in on a double leg and then swap off to 3 different finishes.

Goal setting mistakes

We can think of goal setting mistakes as goal setting that does not meet the previously discussed guidelines. Reviewing how we can violate these ideas will give us a good example of what not to do. Take a look at the following goal setting sins. If you are guilty of any, figure out what you are doing and how you can correct your approach.

Goal setting sins

1) Instead of specific goals, you have non-specific goals. These are ideas that can't be identified. Thoughts such as, "I wish I could do good." "I want to get some recognition." "I want my parents to like what I am doing." are examples of weak, non-specific goals. On the outside these goals look okay, but when you try to define the weak terms, you run into some problems. What is "good"? "Recognition"? How do you get someone to "like" something?

Most goals start out as general ideas. Good goal setters narrow the general down to specific ideas. This can be hard to do. You set yourself up for easy evaluation when you have specific goals. If you don't make the goal, a negative feeling can arise. That is just part of the game we have to get used to. We will not reach every goal. We can only work toward them and adjust when we see that there is a problem.

2) You find yourself dreaming instead of goal setting. You set several unrealistic goals. This is a common problem among young wrestlers. They don't know what they can do, so they guess to the high side and make their goal unobtainable, setting themselves up for failure; not because they don't work to their best ability to reach the goal, but because the goal is impossible to reach. "I should be lifting 200 pounds by next month" is an unrealistic goal for an athlete who is only benching 145 right now. These kids actually are failures at goal setting, not at reaching their goals.

3) You don't set challenging goals. Instead, you make

them too easy. Want to make a goal too hard? Then make it too easy. Yes, you will reach your goal, but then you will become bored and unmotivated. This often contributes to a wrestler stopping workouts all-together.

4) Your goals are not concrete, they are stated in conceptual terms. Setting goals that have steps such as "getting better", "more thorough", "lots of" "I want coach to like me more this year." are not measurable. They can't be meet because no one is sure of the concept.

5) Your goals are not based on what you can do. Instead of being self-referenced, you are other-referenced. You are not someone else, so don't make your goals based on what they can do. A wrestler would be in error if he decided to base his goals on someone else's ability. Milo may be able to climb the rope 10 times in succession, but you need to base your goals on what you can do.

Your goals

Now, let's take some time to look at your goals. Use the following outline and checklist to see if you can make some goals that will actually help you get through the season. State your goal, and then check it against the checklist. If you need to adjust the goal or correct it, that's okay. Setting good goals is an operation that takes time. Don't rush. Look over the guidelines and build your goals for success.

Checklist

Your stated goal:
1. Is it specific?
2. Realistic?
3. Challenging?
4. Concrete?
5. Self-referenced?
6. Have you outlined your baby steps needed to get there? (Short term goals.)

There are a number of situations where wrestlers can use goal setting to help them reach a level of performance that will be acceptable. You can list what you want to accomplish in your preseason workouts. You may want to set goals for practice. Don't forget to design a set of goals for your prematch preparation. We all should also have match goals.

Almost any aspect of your wrestling world can be used as a focal point for setting a goal. You could make some interesting goals for your feet. What about top? Bottom? Post season? Weight class? Making Weight? Lifting Weights? Conditioning?

Evaluate

As you progress in your season stop and take a look at how well you are doing. Look at your short term goals. How are things going? Are you reaching the short term goals? Are you on schedule to reach your next short term goal? Are you still on schedule to reach your final goal?

Adjust

If things are not going as well as you had hoped or predicted, then adjust. It is okay; it's actually better if you read your progress and then change your goals based upon how you are doing. This allows you to handle unexpected developments without having to give up on previous hard work.

Reach out and touch some goals

If things are going well, then take a moment or two to enjoy the success. Predicting the future is hard. Nothing is certain, so setting goals is an uncertain guess at best. If you have the wisdom and discipline enough to set and reach your goals, you need to celebrate. By attaching a positive reward to goal achievement you will reinforce your struggles and encourage yourself or your students to reach more goals.

Learn

Many people think they are failures if they do not reach their goals. This is unrealistic. Goals are future places we are trying to reach. As we all know, no one can control the future. We can only try to do as much as possible to stay headed in the right direction. Weather, other people, luck, fate or something else out of our control can affect even the most perfectly designed plans.

To become philosophical and academic--If goals had to be reached, we would call them rules!

Most people

You will hear your friends, team mates and family talk about what they want to do, how they are going to do it, and what their lifelong dreams are. It is easy to talk about such things, so most people will engage in conversation about the future. Unfortunately, most of these guys will only talk. Very few will be able to carry out the steps necessary to fulfill their wishes.

This is where you can be different. You have the knowledge and hopefully the desire to be able to carry out your dreams.

Conclusion

Goals are different things for different people. Goals can be the destination or final stopping place for your dreams and wishes. Or, goals can be the little steps you are taking to get somewhere.

Goal setting can be a challenge. Most of us have dreams and wishes. By setting goals we are able to organize our pursuit of these dreams.

Goal setting experts have set a list of requirements. They say that goals need to be: 1) specific, 2) realistic, 3) challenging, 4) concrete, and 5) self-referenced.

There are two types of goals: long term and short term. Long term goals are the destination or final place you want to end up. Short term goals are the steps you take along the way to your long term goals.

Good goal setting will center around these steps. Decide what you want to do, and then set your goals. By knowing where you are headed and how to get there, you will have set a good set of plans that will enable you to reach your destination in a quicker and more efficient manner.

Chapter 25

It Ain't
Over,
Until...

Focus: How does one end a season? That's a pretty good question, and it's one we can talk about.

The season's over. Coach has taken up uniforms, completed the inventory, put down the clipboard, and hung up his whistle to dry. The athletes have gone their separate ways, some headed for new sports, some searching for other worthwhile endeavors. Now it's time for coach to hit the golf course, catch up on your rest, or spend some time with the family. It is also time for the wrestlers to move on to their next adventure.

Or is it? The end of the season can present a dilemma for coaches and athletes. Many move from a structured timetable with daily practices and formal schedules to a school-day that now ends with their last class. New activities must be found to fill the time that once was committed to the recently completed season.

Blessing or curse?

This freedom should be a blessing. After all, most of us need some free time to recover from the long hours the world of sports demands. It gives a coach a chance to rejoin the real world, and it also allows students to focus on other commitments such as their social life or academic pursuits. But often there is an empty feeling associated with the completion of a season. What did we accomplish? How well did we really do? Where do we go from here? How do we get there? Many questions need to be answered, and these questions can cause uncertainty and stress if they are not addressed in a timely manner.

What to do?

Conducting a debriefing or closure program may help team members overcome these concerns. Unfortunately, there are no guidelines that explain how a team should end its season. Some coaches choose to end their seasons by holding award ceremonies or year-end banquets. These events celebrate the season and honor the achievements of the preceding year. Other coaches conclude the season without conducting any formal closure. Their teams can resemble a covey of quail that has been flushed from cover. Each member flies off in a different direction, following no set plan, just waiting to regroup sometime in the future.

Wise coaches take the time to tie up these loose ends and set new goals before officially dissolving the group. They make sure each member understands what occurred during the season, what can be done to improve for the future, and how each athlete can accomplish these newly formed goals.

Why bother?

The end of the season is a time of mixed emotions. For some, it is a happy time, a time to enjoy the rewards of reaching desired goals or standards. Winning a certain number of games, setting team records, or performing a personal best can give a team or athlete a feeling of accomplishment that highlights a season. But for many participants, the memories of the season are not so pleasant. High school sports are structured in such a way as to end most seasons on a losing note. Teams that don't make the playoffs often feel as if they were failures, and the tournament season leaves us with only one championship team per classification. This can make it hard for coaches and players to enjoy the season's finale, especially if the season ends with a playoff loss.

Other teams are not exactly sure of how to feel. They have achieved some of their goals, but they are uncertain of their overall performance and are unsure of what to do to improve for next year. This becomes a crucial time for athletes. Many of them need professional guidance in understanding their season and in developing a program or approach that enables them to effectively utilize their off-season time.

Close your season

So, the coaching staff and team members are actually looking for direction to aid them in the upcoming off-season. What can be done? One way of handling these emotions and uncertainties is by installing a system of closure meetings for the team. Coaches and athletes can use these gatherings to clarify the season's results, help remove anxieties, and even plan activities for off-season work. But implementing a program that effectively closes the season is not easy. It takes organization, time, and commitment from both players and coaches.

First there needs to be continued communication and cooperation between the coach and the team members after the season ends. There are several different ways to encourage this. The simplest is to conduct informal interviews among your players. Coaches can check on the players' feelings and attitudes by asking them about the important topics. A more thorough method would be to use a printed form that asks the athletes to evaluate the season. This allows you to compile a set of data that can be easily accessed and analyzed for new ideas, complaints, or suggestions.

Each team has its own personality, but there are several questions that should be included in every evaluation.

Questions to ponder:
*How well did the team do?
*What goals did the team reach?
*What goals did the team fail to reach?
*What are the team's goals for next year?
*How can we reach those goals?
*How did you (the individual) do?

*What worked?
*What didn't?
*What are your goals for next year?
*What do you need to do to reach these goals?

The coaches and athletes should then use these evaluations as an outline for discussions of: 1) where they have been, 2) where they want to go, and 3) what they can do that will help accomplish the goals.

We and I

Two types of meetings should be used to carry out your closure. The first is a team gathering. These group meetings cover the achievements of the team as a whole. The group discusses the team's records, strengths, weaknesses, scheduling, practices and any other topics (injury, weather, illness, etc.) that may have affected the team and its performances.

Individual meetings come next. Private discussions are scheduled between the coach and each athlete. Topics are similar to the group discussions, except that they are geared to meeting the needs of the individual player. It is often a surprise to hear the disclosures that are offered during these meetings as athletes will have many things on their minds that will surprise even the most experienced coach. This is the time coaches can get to know their athletes and build rapport. Coaches and athletes almost always leave these meetings with a better understanding of each other and of what needs to be done to motivate the athletes toward their goals.

Use these meetings to work on positive planning. Avoid becoming emotional, negative, or placing blame. Work to agree upon goals that everyone will find attractive. The coaches have the knowledge, but athletes respond better to goals that they own, so work together to develop the plan, and find a way to *agree on* what needs to be done. As you agree on the goals, write them down. This produces a document that can be used as a schedule, check list, motivational tool, or reminder.

Research into goal setting suggests that goals need to be challenging, but coaches need to be cautious of demanding too much. The athletic arena is just a part of the student's world, and you can set them up for failure by constructing goals that do not meet the needs of their complex lives. Students need to be realistic and base their plans on goals that are challenging, yet with-in reach. Goals that are too easy cause the athlete to become bored. Goals that are too hard or not realistic cause frustration. Either error results in a high drop-out rate.

Plan that vacation

Going through the goal setting process is like planning a vacation. First you must choose your destination; then you can select a direction to follow that gets you there. You can choose from many roads, and the decision is based upon several factors including past performances, personal preferences, and personalities. Athletes often have trouble understanding and applying these concepts to their off-season planning. They are told they need to get 'better', but do not know how to judge what is 'better'. This is where you will be the most help as you assist them in formulating their goals.

Goal setting experts agree that there are certain components that help form successful goals. Effective goals must be:

1) Realistic- Goals should be with-in reach of that particular individual.

2) Specific- Set the desired level of accomplishment. What time, how much weight or how many times? When and where will you workout? With whom?

3) Concrete- Make the goals measurable. Goals such as *get better* are vague and hard to quantify. Concrete goals allow you to know whether you have accomplished your journey or not.

Since you are no longer in a competitive season, it is also a good idea to make the goals self-referenced-- dealing with completing objectives that are designed for each specific athlete. Make sure you reference the goals to activities and skills that can be controlled by the players.

Example

A wrestler might experience proper goal setting like this, "Coach and I have decided that I would be much better if I were stronger. I can bench press about 180 pounds right now. What could I be doing by next fall? About 200 pounds would be a good goal, so I need to figure a way to add 20 pounds. I can lift 2 times a week until school is out. I will work with Coach to develop an upper body program. He is in the weight room on Tuesday and Thursday afternoon. I'll have to schedule my work around that. I will be able to come three times a week during the summer. I have a two week vacation with Dad, but I should be able to catch some work at his place."

This athlete did a good job in selecting and planning his goals. He has made them specific, realistic, self-referenced, and measurable by including: 1) what he wants to accomplish, 2) who he is going to work with, 3) when he is going to work-out, and
4) what he needs to do to carry out the plan. He selected his destination and then developed a good plan that gives direction. Instead of making a weak goal of "I want to get better", he has set his goals on performance-based tasks that make it easy to see if he is moving in the right direction.

Stick to it

Research into program adherence shows that it is hard for most people to continue in a special program for a long period of time. A small group of elite athletes will remain faithful, but a large number of players will lose interest if they are left to work on these plans by themselves. Athletes will find it much easier to adhere to plans if there is a support system in place. Coaches and athletes can work together to install such a program, and there are several ways to enlist support of others.

A buddy system can be a start. Assign your athletes to organized groups. Some coaches like to make groups of three or more. This allows one athlete to miss an activity with-out destroying the group. Design a program that has structure, as some of your athletes will need help with their discipline. But try to keep the program flexible, since many of your players have important commitments that must be worked around. Forcing them to make unnecessary choices can have a negative impact upon your efforts.

Post a checklist, and then follow up with scheduled and unscheduled check-ups. If it becomes apparent that some goals are out of reach, help the students to refocus. Re-evaluate the plan, identify any problems, and then adjust the goals to a new, more obtainable level. Hold follow-up meetings with the athletes to get feedback on the program. Take into consideration any new information, and then try to set some adjusted goals. Even small amounts of success will add positive results to your program, far outshining the negativism or embarrassment of quitting.

Conclusions

The end of the season is a time for evaluation and planning. Coaches and athletes can work together to achieve closure for their season. They should first evaluate the season, and then hold meetings to discuss the findings. These gatherings should reinforce the positive, attempt to adjust and correct problems, and promote growth and skill development. Participants are encouraged to set new goals and then develop a plan based on reaching those goals. Coaches can help by directing the athlete's focus and by providing a support system that assists the athletes in adhering to their plans.

Completing the circle

In reality, the end of the season is just a break. It gives us an opportunity to recover from a long and demanding schedule, but it also allows us time to develop techniques and redirect our thinking in a more leisurely and less stressful atmosphere. With appropriate goal development and good program participation, the off season can be a time for rest, growth, recovery--and tremendous improvement.

So, when your season ends, don't just fly out on your own hoping to find a way to survive until the next season arrives. Get together with your group and make plans to use this time for your enhancement. The end of the season is a time for closing, but it can also be the beginning of future successes. By developing and implementing a good closure system, you and your athletes will have a better idea of what has been done and what is expected of them in the future.

If it ain't over... it is close to it! US Olympian Michael Foy shows outstanding back-arch technique as he completes this toss.

Photo courtesy of USA Wrestling and Michael Foy

Chapter 26

Mental Skills Program for Wrestling

░░

Focus: Experts suggest that coaches design and use organized and systematic programs to help their athletes learn the mental skills.

░░

It is match time and excitement fills the air. Each wrestler has worked hard learning moves, conditioning, and making weight. The team is prepared and the plans have been covered, but there is still a feeling of nervousness. Some athletes appear anxious, while others seem unmotivated or flat. How will the team perform?

Many factors influence performances, and that makes it hard to predict how someone will do in a match or tournament. Often we see athletes failing to reach the level of perfection they obtained in their previous efforts. What causes these fluctuations? How much do mental factors affect performances? What can be done to gain better control of performances?

In an attempt to address these questions, our staff looked into implementing a mental skills program (MSP) for our wrestling team. There were no standard or packaged programs available, so we chose to develop a system of our own. Ideas were borrowed from many sources, and concepts were researched and developed to fit our individuals' styles and our team's needs.

Our system works on two levels: the *developmental* level, and the *intervention* level. Each level has its own groups, goals, and procedures.

In the *developmental level*, mental skills are introduced to the whole team. Different types of stress are identified, and the athletes are exposed to a buffet of coping strategies. Athletes are introduced to, and practice mental skills that will enable them to prepare for the pressures of practice, matches, and the long season. This phase of the MSP is neither therapy nor counseling, but a series of discussions on ways for athletes to handle stress.

Level two, the *intervention portion* of our program, is where we work with athletes who are experiencing anxiety, motivational, or personal problems. It involves small group and individual work and deals with correcting performance problems the athletes may be experiencing.

Teaching skills

The teaching of psychological skills closely resembles that of physical skills, as many of the methods and techniques are similar. We introduce each skill in a simple form, master it, and then proceed to more complex usage.

In level one we introduce concepts such as *positive self-talk*, *motivation*, *arousal*, and *goal setting*. We discuss *state anxiety* (how some people get nervous because of what is happening), and *trait anxiety* (how some competitors are naturally more nervous than others). We also discuss situational *strategies* like when to choose top, when to release the man, what to do with a big lead in the last period, when to use a desperation move, or other situations that wrestlers could encounter in a match.

We present the information to the team in a matter-of-fact style. A coach might start the discussion by saying, "Sometimes athletes get nervous before a match. Here are some of the things successful wrestlers have done to overcome those nervous feelings."

Another discussion may start with, "What should a wrestler think about when he steps onto the mat for match? We want our wrestlers to be thinking of motion and attacking their man. What move are you thinking?" The team has a short dialog on ideas that have and have not worked for different individuals.

Level two is handled differently. We have discovered that some athletes have trouble controlling their thoughts and feelings. We work to teach these wrestlers how to become calm, direct themselves towards a goal, and to build self-confidence. *Focus, relaxation,* and *visualization* are the major techniques we teach this group. The three skills are introduced to the athletes; then they are practiced as specific, individual skills.

Mental skills

Focusing is the ability to align thoughts to a specific idea or goal. It allows us to zero in on the desired topic while ignoring unwanted input. The athletes are taught to select the appropriate ideas, or topics to think about during competitions, and to concentrate on those idea. We encourage the wrestlers to concentrate on physical skills such as motion, set-ups, penetration, and their favorite moves. We urge them to focus on things they can control. This allows the athletes to keep a clear head and remain task oriented while ignoring distractions.

Relaxation is employed as an aid in controlling tension. It is a skill the athletes can use to limit activation. Students are taught to relax by using an adaptation of the progressive relaxation method, where students tense different muscle groups and then relax them to remove the tension. During relaxation drills the coach is a facilitator, guiding the athletes through the steps by calling out the muscle groups or by suggesting peaceful settings for the athletes to focus on.

Relaxation is practiced on a regular basis, and many of the athletes learn to relax without the flexing. Students learn to focus on their body, identify areas of excessive tension, and then try to relax the tension away. They also use the relaxation to prepare for visualization, to help control their thoughts, and as a aid in sleeping. Athletes are encouraged to use the relaxation any time they feel nervous or anxious. Many athletes become so skilled at this that the coach's role in relaxation is reduced to merely getting the session started.

Visualization is the process of picturing thoughts and sensations in one's mind. It can be compared to controlled daydreaming. We introduce this skill by asking the students to close their eyes and picture simple ideas, scenes, or thoughts. We then ask athletes to picture themselves in action versus a recognizable opponent. The athletes are encouraged to do more than just "see" the action. They are requested to "feel it". Specific moves are suggested and the wrestler tries to experience positive endings to his vision. Many of our athletes report vivid experiences such as noting the color of uniforms and even describing the referee. As with relaxation, the coach is a guide who directs the members by suggesting scenes or settings.

After the basics of these skills are mastered we begin to combine them into a mental skills triad of focusing, relaxation, and visualization. By combining these three skills we seem to achieve greater results than by using each skill individually. The relaxation enhances the visualization which helps to heighten the focus. We intensify the experience by asking the athletes to envision specific situations such as being behind, riding a foe for the last seconds, performing before a huge crowd, or maybe needing a pin to win. We also lengthen the duration of the sessions. We note different rates of learning and different levels of mastery, but almost every wrestler reports improvement with practice.

Program's structure

We introduce the program to our team in the early part of the year. We point out the importance of mental training and expose our athletes to the vocabulary that will be used. Athletes learn what it means to focus, self-talk, analyze feelings, and to recover from unexpected events. Terms such as visualization, relaxation, imagery, and stress are discussed. We talk openly about mental skills and try to make each athlete see the program as a part of the sport and not an outside entity.

Early mental skills practices are short and on an

educational level. Level one includes all of our athletes. This group receives its mental training during regular practice sessions.

Level two is the intervention group. For this group we select wrestlers who many be showing some inconsistencies. We watch for 1) match performance that is not consistent with the performance achieved in practice, 2) extreme premeet nervousness (over-activation) 3) match frustration, 4) loss of control in performance, 5) temper episodes, or, 6) general signs of unhappiness. These students are interviewed informally. We listen for comments dealing with anxiety, fear of failure, excitability, or other negative concerns the athlete may be feeling or showing.

We explain the program and then offer the wrestlers a chance to join. We then begin small group work with the athletes who choose to participate. Most of them appear to enjoy the meetings. (Athletes who don't are allowed to withdraw.) We have one meeting a week for the first month, and then we schedule two short meetings per week as the schedule enters the tournament stretch.

The procedure is simple. After practice the athletes are assembled in a quiet place and allowed to cool down. The coach guides them through a short relaxation period; this helps athletes to focus by introducing a mental skills topic. After the athletes have relaxed they are encouraged to begin visualizing a scene. Each wrestler chooses his own scene and continues the experience for fifteen to twenty minutes. The athletes are requested to focus on different scenes such as pre-match drilling techniques, winning, performing well against an opponent, or just having fun wrestling. A group discussion follows in which the athletes talk about their experiences and how the exercise affected them. After completion of the activity the wrestlers dress-in and prepare to go home.

Students who request additional information, or attention are counseled individually. Topics such as time management, weight reduction, peer pressures, grades, and girl friends are discussed. If serious problems appear we refer the students to our school counselor. Although coaches are often forced into the capacity, we must remember: We are not counselors!

Results

Some results are immediate and easy to see. After participating in group sessions the level two athletes are relaxed and in a rested state. Most of them believe that they have better control of their emotions, and many request additional sessions. Athletes in both groups start talking more about the mental side of sport using the psychological terms and asking questions that include the mental skills vocabulary. We have received a wide range of acceptance of the program, and we have no problems with negative labels on any of our participating athletes.

We have also noticed a different attitude in the wrestling room. Practices are more intense, yet more fun, than before we started the program. Anytime a drill begins to drag we inject a mental skills moment and redirect the focus. During these moments we discuss a term, a match situation, or sometimes we conduct a short activity. Visitors are often amused by our 'walking circle massage', where the team forms a circle and walks around the mat, each man massaging the shoulders of the man in front of him while the coach tells an interesting story or makes general comments. Coaches like being able to maintain motivation and intensity without the conflicts that often arise when cutting weight or working near maximum levels.

Long term results are more difficult to document. There is no hard physical evidence, but coaches and athletes perceive a difference in performances. The wrestlers are more positive about their contests. They also appear to be in greater control of their levels of activation. It is not uncommon to see a group of wrestlers laying beside the mat in a focused, relaxed state, while hundreds of fans scream at the wrestling taking place.

Often, after the match, the wrestlers discuss their visions, examine what they experienced and how it affected their matches. More than once we have heard a wrestler tell another, "It was just like I saw it in practice!"

The program allows us to teach the mental side of sports to all of our athletes and to devote extra time to students who need it. This mental training compliments our physical training and fits in well with our philosophy of developing a well rounded student: one who can perform well and excel in athletics, academics, and society.

Cost of implementation

We have incurred no monetary costs in operating the MSP. The major expenditure were involved with changing practice philosophies, finding the information to use, and allocating the time to include the program.

Our coaching staff found sport psychology material readily available in books and periodicals, and we used that information to develop much of our program. We then organized the program to make efficient use of our time. The educational phase is incorporated within the daily practices. We discuss the methods and talk strategies while the athletes are warming up, stretching, jumping rope, or cooling down. This is perfect as no wrestling time is 'lost'.

The intervention sessions do pose a slight inconvenience as we have elected to hold them after practice. We were pleased to see that the athletes will stay the extra time to enjoy the benefits.

We believe we have developed a program that is effective and worthwhile. It is sound in theory, application, and time utilization, and it is also financially feasible. Our athletes have enjoyed much success while using the MSP, and our teams respond well to high caliber competition. We believe the positive attitudes and results more than justify the time and effort spent in the program.

Chapter 27

Closing

Focus: Just what did we say? Let's have some final comments on the ideas and theories that we discussed and covered.

Does it feel like you have taken a long trip through a mental skills dictionary? I hope so. And I hope you were able to pick up on some techniques and methods that will help you perform better and enjoy your matches more.

You may want to look into the ideas we covered to find which ones will help you the most in your competitive life. We offered so many ideas that it will probably be hard to recall all of them. There really is no way that you could, so don't worry about it. The best thing to do is to go back and read over the chapters that you feel will help you the most. Learn the ideas and concepts so well that they become part of the way you think, and then forget them. That way, you will not spend any extra energy thinking about the material when you should be focusing on your performances.

Why don't you take a moment and try to recall some of the major ideas you read. Remember terms such as: focus, motivation, self-talk, activation, stress, visualization, and goals. Try to organize these words into a frame of mind that will help you understand and control your competitive self. (What ideas or which chapter helped you the most?)

So, how did you do? Do you remember a lot of the material? Did the review help get the ideas down into a simple form? Do you think you are ready to try some of the ideas with a fellow wrestler, athlete, or yourself?

We can practice a little and see how you would do. Let me introduce you to *Wilburfer Widenback*. He is your normal first year wrestler. He knows a good number of moves, but he has never really been helped to understand the ideas behind performance psychology. Listen to his stories and help him with some wise information that you may have picked up while cruising the pages of this book!

You're the sport psychologist

Let's see what you would do if you were asked to help a wrestler enhance his performance or overcome a difficulty. Read the following scenarios and then make a plan to help the athlete or to fix the wrestler's problem. It should be interesting. We will say that you are on Wilburfer's team and your coach has asked you to be Wilburfer's mentor. Make your best recommendations and help our boy do better. You will find recommended readings included with every scene.

Wilburfer has a match tonight. He is sitting by you waiting to make weight. He tells you a lot--really more than you want to know, but he is on your team, so you must help him. Listen, ponder the statements, and then tell him what you think will help. Remember, Wilburfer is a good guy. He just hasn't reached your level of understanding or wisdom.

1. Wilburfer is a little nervous in appearance. He has been pacing for about 20 minutes. He looks to you and says, **"I'm so nervous. My stomach is in knots, my hands are cold, and I can't sit still. What can I do? I feel so uptight.?"**

2. He follows your suggestion, but comes back in about 10 minutes and says, **"I'm thinking. He is suppose to be pretty good. I heard he has a tremendous headlock. Heck, you know I'm a sucker for a headlock. He'll kill me. And their team is so tough. I just can't get it out of my mind."**

3. You see Wilburfer getting ready to wrestle. He is about to walk toward the mat from behind your bench area. You ask how's he doing, and what he's going to do. He says, **"Oh, I don't know. I haven't thought**

about that. Coach told me he was a thrower--
That I'm not suppose to tie up. I'm going to
follow Coach's directions. I'm not going to
tie up. That is all I have been thinking
about."

4. To your amazement, and also to your credit,
Wilburfer is hanging in there. He is battling tough and
has scored. He is up by one point when he drops in for a
double leg, loses his balance, and has to push his
opponent out of bounds to keep from giving up a
takedown. They roll onto the floor and get up. **To your
horror, the ref makes a terrible call that
changes the score against your team.** He gives
the other man a takedown, although there was clearly no
control. Wilburfer is shocked. His feelings are hurt and
he is confused. Coach takes out to the table to argue the
call. Wilburfer looks to you and shakes his head. There
are 30 seconds left. Wilburfer is down by one. He is just
shaking his head saying, "No, No, No. It wasn't a
takedown. Why did he do that? What can I do?"

At practice Wilburfer comes up to you and has
several comments. Help him by suggesting solutions to
his worries and concerns.

5). Wilburfer is a good bit overweight. He is talking
about **getting a sauna suit and 3 pairs of
sweats, and then rolling up in the mat to
make weight.** He doesn't want to skip tonight's pizza
buffet with his buddies. He knows he can cut a bunch of
weight tomorrow if he can just get hot enough.

Wilburfer confides to you:

6) **"I watch the demonstrations, but I just
can't seem to understand the moves. I just
don't feel like I know what he means. How
can I learn them if I don't get the idea?"**

He says:

7) **"I'm not penetrating into my man.
Coach says that I need to get in closer. What
does he mean? I just can't turn that corner**

on my high crotch. What can I do to help me learn to step in closer and turn my corner?"

8) "Last night I couldn't sleep. I wasn't able to get some thoughts out of my mind. I keep seeing myself shoot in, but I wouldn't finish my move. I just lay there and watched myself shoot in, again and again. I wish I knew how to see myself be successful."

9) "How can I get ready to wrestle my next match? I have problems starting about two days before the match. I get lost at the gym. I mean, I'm not really lost, it's just I don't know what to do between matches."

10) "Coach was talking about goals today. What did he mean by set some performance goals? And he said goals needed to be a list of things for them to be effective. What was that list and what did he mean? What is a performance goal? An outcome goal? Can you help me with that stuff?"

11) "Man, you are so smart. Where did you learn all of this stuff?" says Wiberfur. "Where can I find wrestling information like you have been talking about? I've looked in the bookstores and had my parents checking for me, but there is not much out there. I want to be the best I can be. Where can we get some books, tapes or other junk that will help us learn?"

12) Someone knows you have read a book on sport psychology for wrestling. They ask you to take a group through relaxation. What would you do? How would you start? What would you say?

13) You do so well with the relaxation that coach asks you to take 3 of your team members through a visualization session. How would you start? What would you do? What would you say?

14) How does a wrestler learn to drill? What would you do to help the athletes learn and understand the importance of drilling?

15) Every wrestler will need to know how to choose top, bottom, neutral, or defer. It is a choice that is made in every match. Teach Wilburfer and your team mates the strategies behind making that choice.

How did you do?

By now you should have a good grip on many of the mental skills techniques. It will take some time before you feel comfortable using them with other people. Just make sure you start to use them with yourself. You can do this by simply thinking about the ideas and making a little speech to yourself.

Choose any topic we discussed, apply it to your wrestling, and then think about how you want to react in that situation. Make your thoughts into a little speech, memorize them, then forget it.

You have made it to the end. Good! That puts you ahead of most wrestlers. You now know about mental skills, preparing for competition, and designing your mental skills programs. These skills should help you reach a new level in your athletic life.

The idea of mental training is not new. Many different groups have been using mental skills for centuries. The "newness" to this idea is in having an open, organized program that is taught to athletes and coaches. The key to your continuing success will be in whether you are able to incorporate the ideas from this book into your athletic life. There are several things you need to look into before you make a decision on how you will use these skills.

1) Decide how mental skills fits your athletic needs. What do you need? If you are an athlete, think about how the ideas fit your special personality. Where have you had problems? What do you want help in accomplishing? How can you use these skills?

Coaches, think about how these ideas fit your coaching philosophies. How would you use them? Do you have athletes who need this type of information? Who? What is the best way to get them the information? How will you design your mental skills training program?

2) Practice the techniques. Use them at practice and at home. It only takes a second or two to focus on a particular topic and practice it. It basically takes the desire to do it. The actual practice is not that hard.

3) Make them part of your life. These skills will help you in several areas of your life. They are not wrestling specific. You can transfer the skills to other sports. Most of my clients tell me that these skills also help them at home, at school, and on tests.

4) Live by the ideas. Once you learn the concepts, you can live the ideas!

5) Forget them.. The final step in mental skills mastery is to learn the skills so well that you forget them. Spend no conscious effort in thinking about any of these concepts. You have made them part of your thinking and part of your living.

I invite you to drop me a line about any of the ideas put forth in this work. I am usually pretty good about getting back to people. I also would like to hear your stories. I am constantly writing about performance and I need examples of real life events, so fire those pencils up. Make comments. Tell me what you liked or hated.

Sharing ideas and thought can be the most satisfying thing we do. I tried to help you by sharing the little bit of knowledge I that I have. Now, you can help me by sharing your knowledge.

Thanks again, and

Wrestle to win!

Resources

I have quoted and referred you to some of these works. The others have influenced me or impacted me through their teachings. If you are interested in mental skills, these writings will give you some insight and knowledge in the area.

Books

Coaching Young Athletes. Rainer Martens. (1987). Human Kinetics Publishers. Champaign, IL.

Coaches Guide To Sport Psychology. Rainer Martens. (1988). Human Kinetics Publishers. Champaign, IL.

Fighting Invisible Tigers. Earl Hipp. (1985). Free Spirit Publishing. Minneapolis, MN.

Flow. Mihaly Csikszentmihalyi. (1990). Harper Trade Books.

Foundations of Sport and Exercise Psychology. Robert Weinberg and Daniel Gould. (1995). Human Kinetics. Champaign, IL.

Lure the Tiger from The Mountains. Gao Yuan. (1991). Simon and Schuster. New York, NY.

Inner Game of Tennis. Timothy Gallaway. (1989). Bantam Books. New York, NY.

In the Zone. Rhea White. (1995). Penguin Books. New York, NY.

In Pursuit Of Excellence. Terry Orwell. (1990). Leisure Press. Champaign, IL.

Introduction to Psychology. Charles Morris. (1992). Prentiss Hall.

Mental Toughness Training for Sports. James E. Loehr. (1986). Stephen Greene Press.

Peak Performance. Charles Garfield. (1984). Warner Books. New York, NY.

Psychology of Injury. John Heil. (1993). Human Kinetics. Champaign, IL.

Rip Roaring Reads For Reluctant Teen Readers. Sherman, G. & Ammon, B. (1993). California: Libraries Unlimited.

Sport Psychology Interventions. Shane Murphy. (1995) Human Kinetics. Champaign, IL.

The Art of War, by Sun Tzu. Translated by Yuan Shibing. (1990). Sterling Publishing. New York, NY.

The Inner Athlete. Dan Millman. (1994). Stillpoint Publishing. Walpole, NH.

The Mental Athlete. Kay Porter and Judy Foster. (1986). Ballantine Books. New York, NY.

The Mental Game. James E. Loehr. (1990). Penguin Press. New York, NY.

Unlimited Power. Tony Robbins. (1986). Ballantine Books. New York, NY.

Winning. Stuart Walker. (1990). Norton Publishing. New York, NY.

Coach Hendrix listens to World Cup Champion Matt Ghaffari discuss his "perfect match plans" at the US Olympic Training Center.

Coach Beasey Hendrix

Education Specialist Degree, West Georgia College. 1992.
Masters Degree (psychology), West Georgia College. 1989.
BA (communications), University Alabama. 1982.

Accomplishments:

US Olympic Team Trials Finalist. (1976, 1980).
Wrestling USA National Hall of Fame.
WUSA National Assistant Coach of the Year.
USA Wrestling Gold Level Coaches Certification.
USA Wrestling Bronze and Silver Level Coaches Certification.
WUSA Georgia Man of the Year.
USWF Alabama Wrestling Man of the Year.
Georgia Athletic Coaches Association State Assistant Coach of the Year. (4X).
GACA Area Assistant Coach of the Year. (6X).
GACA Area Coach of the Year (Cross Country). (6X).
Who's Who Among America's Teachers. (1990-94).
USA Wrestling Bronze Level Coaches Instructor.
USAW Silver Level Coaches College Instructor.
National H. S. Athletic Coaches Convention Speaker.
Consultant: USA Freestyle and Greco World Teams.
Consultant to numerous college and university teams.
Authored more than 25 mental skills articles for over a dozen magazines.
His teams and clubs have produced over 20 All-Americans, over 30 individual state champions.
Mental skills consultant to Olympic athletes and World Champions in several sports.
Named "Coach", "Man", or "Assistant Coach of the Year" over 2 dozen times by 7 different organizations.

Notes from your readings

Order form for books

Please send me _____ copies of :

Wrestle To Win!
Be smart. Be Ready.

I have enclosed $13.95 plus $3.00 shipping and handling (Georgia residents add 5% tax) to:

High Performance Athletics
P.O. Box 669364
Marietta, Georgia 30066

Name_____

Address_____

City/State/Zip_____ _____ _____

Phone number:_____-_____-_____

If you have any questions about techniques or ideas presented in **Wrestle To Win!,** or want to tell me about things you do, feel free to write me at:
P.O.Box 669364
Marietta, GA 30066

Another book by Coach Hendrix:
Sports Psychs
Yes, I can!
Mental Skills For Athletes

Coach Hendrix identifies and organizes mental skills for athletes into an easy 8 step program. Due to be published in September, 1996.